PENGUIN BOOKS

WORD FROM WORMINGFORD

'It takes a delicate touch to define the beauty and bitterness of the English landscape ... Ronald Blythe has one of the surest touches of country life I have ever had the pleasure to read. His *Word from Wormingford*, chronicles of a parish year, combines prose of breathtaking beauty with a sage and reflective spirit. His land is the land of Constable and Nash; his fields, the fields of John Clare and Thomas Hardy' Christina White, *Catholic Herald*

'Blythe is a vivid and entertaining chronicler of the bizarre and the forgotten ... He inhabits an almost Hardyesque world' Jeremy Lewis, *Sunday Times*

'Blythe lives with a deep, authentic sense of wonder – and if it sometimes drives him rather wildly hither and thither, it certainly helps him to follow his master in inspiring that " necessary happiness and delight"' Derwent May, *The Times Literary Supplement*

'Gentle reader, there is a treat in store. A gift of clear water from a deep well. Sweetly, oh so sweetly, do we slip into the poet's pocket. In *Akenfield*, the book with which Ronald Blythe made his name, we saw what we once were. In *Word from Wormingford*, we see what we hope we may still remain. We want – we need – to believe in this tranquil world' Elisabeth Luard, *The Times*

'Delightful ... In the rich gossip and fierce fighting that at once divides and unites the community we have an unblinking witness' Jasper Gerard, *Express on Sunday*

Ronald Blythe has written poetry, short stories, history and literary criticism, much of it reflecting his East Anglian background. His first book, the novel *A Treasonable Growth*, was published in 1960. *Akenfield*, his remarkable evocation of rural change, much of which he had witnessed, appeared in 1969. It was followed by *The View in Winter*, a study of old age. *The Age of Illusion* and *Writing in a War*, an anthology, contain further personal assessments of Britain's recent past. *From the Headlands*, Ronald Blythe's collected essays, was published in 1982 and *Divine Landscapes* was published by Viking in 1986. Penguin also publish *Private Words: Letters and Diaries from the Second World War*. His work has been translated and filmed and has received a number of literary awards.

Ronald Blythe has also edited *The Penguin Book of Diaries*, and edited and introduced a number of volumes in the Penguin Classics, including *Emma*, by Jane Austin, William Hazlitt's *Selected Writings*, *The Awkward Age* by Henry James and *Far From the Madding Crowd* by Thomas Hardy.

WORD FROM WORMINGFORD

A PARISH YEAR

RONALD BLYTHE

With illustrations by John Nash

PENGUIN BOOKS

PENGUIN BOOKS

Published by the Penguin Group
Penguin Books Ltd, 27 Wrights Lane, London W8 5TZ, England
Penguin Putnam Inc., 375 Hudson Street, New York, New York 10014, USA
Penguin Books Australia Ltd, Ringwood, Victoria, Australia
Penguin Books Canada Ltd, 10 Alcorn Avenue, Toronto, Ontario, Canada M4V 3B2
Penguin Books (NZ) Ltd, 182–190 Wairau Road, Auckland 10, New Zealand

Penguin Books Ltd, Registered Offices: Harmondsworth, Middlesex, England

First published by Viking 1997
Published in Penguin Books 1998
3 5 7 9 10 8 6 4 2

Printed in England by Clays Ltd, St Ives plc

For Peter-Paul and Kate Nash

In
memory of
ELIZABETH wife of
JOHN ALLINGTON

Introduction

This is the calendar of a Reader who happens to be a writer. It was originally published weekly in *Church Times* over the years 1993–6 and I am grateful to the editor Paul Handley for his permission to make a book of it. Wormingford, Mount Bures and Little Horkesley are a united benefice of ancient parishes, each one, as such places tend to be, subtly different in its worship. Wormingford is on the River Stour and was the home of John Constable's uncles and aunts and cousins whom he called 'the Wormingford folk'. It was also the home of my old friend John Nash, who painted here for half a century, and of his wife Christine who taught everybody dancing, acting and music. John Nash and his wife Christine were my close friends for many years, and I came to live in their old farmhouse at Wormingford after their deaths. The artist himself began painting in and around this Stour Valley village in 1929 and came to know every inch of it. He liked to describe himself as an 'artist-plantsman' and his botanical understanding of the riverside landscape equalled that which inspired his work. He and Christine lie by the churchyard hedge, a few steps from John Constable's farmer relations. The 'mount' of Mount Bures is a Norman earthworks high above the River Colne, and the church there has always seemed to me to contain a unique kind of sanctity, hard to put into words. The medieval church at Little Horkesley was turned to dust at 9.50 p.m. on 21 September 1940 by a German landmine. Earlier that same day a young RAF officer and his bride were married in it. He was killed six months later. A new church was built on the spot in 1958.

Each village has a pub and there is a Church of England School which serves all three. They stand in hilly agricultural scenery and between two river locations which are famous in English art, Gainsborough's Sudbury and Constable's East Bergholt.

Advent

A spring feeds the old house as it ultimately feeds the river. Now and then I visit it under the elder and blackberry copse, and see silver beads trickling across dark earth. Just a few steps on they are a runnel, then a gravelly stream, then water in a well, then water under my roof. Its purity was famous not so long ago for the making of beer. What I cannot use overflows into a horse-pond, into the lake, into the Stour. I hear them as I write, as I wake, the spring, the stream, the river, adding to each other in their catchment, their water-table. So it has been for centuries.

Inside me, just as incessant, runs what the experimental novelists of the inter-war years recognized as a 'stream of consciousness', a description by the philosopher William James of that unstoppable flow of thoughts and feelings which runs through all our heads. Virginia Woolf was able to drive her stream of consciousness into all kinds of readable directions. The clergy are only too aware of the wastage of ideas, of inspiration, of words. How they stream past too quick for pen or tape. There is no getting them down, not the best of them. Writers too are often in a quandary due to knowing that what gets on to the page is no more than a sad shadow of what, that very minute, had been pouring through their brains. William James paid homage to this marvellous 'stream of thought, of subjective life'. He said that, although its usual metaphor is that of a stream, there was an irregularity in it which also reminded him of a bird's life, with its flights and perchings. So every now and then the divine process does hesitate long enough for us

3

to seize something from it. But these must be fragments of 'one protracted consciousness, one unbroken stream'.

The religious mind has, more than any other mind than that of poet and artist, tried hard to navigate this stream, to follow it, to chart it. It sometimes sees its current as a help to discursive prayer – meditation. I see it as a tantalizing part of an intelligence which first allows me to see, and then whisks out of sight, all the things I would like to talk about on Sunday, or set down in Chapter One. It is bitterly cold and might be mid-winter. Several oaks have shed their leaves in a night, the rest creak. The sheep move up the hill field in dense bundles. The horses breathe plumes. It is Advent and my consciousness revives, rushes ahead of manageable thinking, which is all very exciting but not much use when one has to preach for ten minutes.

St Andrew

A freezing coming for St Andrew, our village's patron. Hoar-frost and light sprinklings of snow have delineated the land, accenting the autumn drilling, giving every twig its due. The recently dense copse is now a lattice through which I can watch the hares on the far field. They are not skylarking but thump about heavily, 'frawn 'o cold', as they say here. This would have been the time for one of my old friend John Nash's window pictures. Now and then I come across one in a gallery, sometimes with glazing-bars but usually just framed in the window-space, views of the icy garden with trailing pheasants, of the neighbouring farms, of his loved seedheads and floral

senescence. Inside work, as he called it. Winter work for every pane in the house. His first and greatest snow picture is 'Over the Top', a recollection of himself and seventy-nine other soldiers in action near Cambrai in 1917. He and a dozen mates survived. The khaki against snow also survived on his palette, to be used for the rest of his long life for weeks such as this.

A window in a painting draws my attention away from what is happening in the room, the Annunciation, Jerome translating in thin sunlight, some horror connected with martyrdom. The Italian masters are always saying, 'Take a look outside.' Like so many others who share the fairly recent passion for landscape, I have pored over Julian's famously scanty views of medieval Norfolk seen, of course, from her window on the world. She saw hazels which one cannot see now, so they are to be put back into the picture by Dr Ellis Roberts, *Corylus avellana*, or 'that which exists now and forever, because God loves it'.

The proto-Christmas card has arrived, Frans de Momper's 'Village in Winter', where there are a hundred seventeenth-century windows looking out on the anti-hypothermian revels of Flanders to see skating, huggings, snowballing, anything to keep the circulation going. I can hear the river cracking, the rushes whipping, the crows protesting around the spire, and I am relieved to contrast this cold snap with that cold season, in which one had to play to stay alive. The windows there are black holes which say, 'Go out to get warm.'

Quite my favourite window mishap is in Acts 20. Poor young Eutychus goes down in Christian history as the first man to doze off during a sermon. He is sitting in the window listening to Paul preaching when he falls asleep and tumbles three storeys to the ground. Paul, ever practical, rushes down to resuscitate him, then returns to continue preaching until the *morning*. As for Eutychus, who cannot have been the hero of many sermons, his friends 'were not a little comforted' to have him back alive. This high window was in Troas, just up the lane from Troy, and it looked out on what had once been Helen's prospect. Winding up at last, Paul sets sail for Mitylene, city of great men.

Nicholas Ferrar

The girls are coming to talk me through the Guided Walk and I rise early to get a good fire going. There is nothing to equal a big blaze on the hearth on a winter's morning. The kindling makes its xylophonic music as it tumbles about, the chimney prepares itself for a roar and the split willow for incandescence. I am taken back to Dorothy Sewart's heroic hearth in north Cornwall on which a whole faggot would be tossed as nonchalantly as we lesser fire-makers might toss a spent match. But then Miss Sewart was behind the door when cautions and niceties were given out. Being told at twenty-five that she had not long to live, she decided to live recklessly and was continuing to live even more recklessly at eighty-five. Her little house lay at the bottom of a funnel of rocks and trees. Steep steps and flimsy handrails brought us down to it. Wild waters churned below it and the word which rang around in our heads as we made our way to tea was 'impossible'. But here she had dwelt ever since some 'tom-fool doctor' had pronounced her death sentence. She was a famous nurserywoman specializing in flowerless chamomile which produced delicately scented lawns. Adverts for it appeared in the best country magazines, 'Treneague Chamomile' which perfumed one's feet. My hosts the poet and his wife lived above her on the high ground and were kept in their place. Myself as the winter guest had no place at all and I sat where I was told to and knew when not to ask questions. In any case it was Miss Sewart's glorious hearth which spoke all that was necessary. It was a sparking, spitting cave and part of one of the most beautiful cottage rooms I have ever seen. A white lumpen-walled room with a slate floor and no soft furniture, which smelled of cake and the chamomile offshoots (£1.90 a hundred).

'Where was it you said you come from? Suffolk?' A pitying look. The poet and his wife, who had emigrated from this county, gloated. They spoke of ferocious east winds and a bitterness which Miss Sewart wouldn't believe. She sent me out for 'more sticks', meaning half a hedge to cast into the inferno. There is nothing to compare with lavish simplicity. Outside, hartstongue dripped and sodden sheep wailed.

The poet's other near neighbour was Mr Bates who, when still young, may have heard of Logan Pearsall Smith's confession, 'People say that life is the thing, but I prefer reading' – for this was all he did from dawn to dusk. Nieces fed him with library books as sparrows fed their gape-mouthed chicks, by the fireside or in the summer garden. Here before our very eyes, and flagrantly, two souls 'lived unto themselves', as Hazlitt put it.

St Nicholas

Thin sunshine continues to filter a surprising warmth over our Advent fields and we are told that there has been nothing like it since sixteen-something. So we bask in the rarity of this mildness. Billy's calendar tells her that there will be lambing on Christmas Day, Anthea's calendar tells her that it is less than a week to her wedding-day, Barrie's calendar warns him that the annual Bellringers' Dinner at the Crown is upon him, and has everyone ticked his preference, turkey or beef? Little cardboard windows in the kitchen calendar have to be prised open each Advent morning. At Wormingford we sing 'O come, O come, thou Dayspring bright!' and at Horkesley there is an entire service of pleading carols. They have (said Percy Dearmer) a dancing origin, 'expressing the manner in which the ordinary man at his best understood the ideas of his age'. The extraordinary women too, I find myself amending, as I remember Elizabeth Poston.

The toys of faith are never quite put away. This notion occurs to me as we wander cross-country to Hadleigh, taking the twisting boyhood route from River Stour to River Brett, an up-hill and down-dale journey along lanes with towering banks and still a few flowers. At this mild rate the winter wheat will be cut in March. This is the way I used to travel with John Nash. Now and then he would brake the Triumph Herald to take stock of some excitement in the landscape – 'That's a good bit' – and tucking its detail into his head until it could be put into his sketchbook.

And so to Hadleigh church, which could be called an almanac for the entire English religious experience for those who know how to turn the page. There dangling from the spire is the angelus bell which told the medieval ploughmen to call it a day, there is the room in which in 1833 the young rector Hugh Rose inaugurated the Tractarian Movement and from which in 1554 the old rector Rowland Taylor began the horrible *via dolorosa* which led to his burning on the common. There too, among the sprawling arches, is where two of the translators of the Authorized Version sat as children.

'I'll put the lights on for you,' says the lady who would have been doing the vases, only it is Advent, a fearful time, and one which the Church must meet in all its gaunt reality.

Second in Advent

Every now and then it happens, the loner dies and the sociable are made to feel unsociable. Why, how, is it possible for a man on his own (they are speaking about old Mr Bartholomew) to depart on his own? And who was he, apart from being the quiet face at the bungalow window which stared past our waves? Half a dozen of us from the church stood proxy for his non-existent family and friends and falling earth wrote finis to yet one more solitary achievement, miracle even, of keeping oneself to oneself. As none of us is allowed to leave it at that, a kind of having, long ago, 'seen something nasty in the woodshed' excuse has been made for his withdrawal from us. Which is that he had a glimpse of Belsen.

I doubt if this is the answer, or if such rural reclusivity is to be explained. There cannot be many country priests who have not met with it. I once mourned a hermit, as they dubbed him locally, whom I had never so much as glimpsed through a pane. It was in wintry Cornwall and a poet friend had said, 'Do you mind coming with me? We shall be the only ones.' A gale tore through the steep churchyard. This old man had been unlucky in love, it was put about. 'As a matter of fact,' said the poet, 'he died with his nose in a book.' An element of special sadness accompanied us home, all the same. The December light failed and I thought of shadow being a metaphor for protection in the Bible.

There is a line in the RV translation of Psalm 68 which has often intrigued me – 'He setteth the solitaries in families'. So would we, I suspect, and, given half a chance, make everybody unhappy. What I would like to know about all the loners I haven't known is how their years passed. There they stretch, from my boyhood on, the usually pleasant faces that might say

'Good morning', but never 'come in'. That 'I' of the Psalmist is the I of a man who is much alone. His Temple Songs sprang from the unique silence which surrounds the solitary. Those who ask nothing of nobody until the undertaker calls are a dreadful worry to village Christians.

Seasonal Happiness

It is snowing. Flakes are building up on the flowers and melting on the warm backs of beasts, leaving a sodden gloss. Max looks out in disgust before selecting the softest, warmest chair in the kitchen in which to winter. His green eyes close in prayer as he thanks God for creating men to wait on cats. It is not as cold as the forecasters insist but very wild and dark. The study is covered with letters from the Western Front which are waiting to go into a book. One is blotchy and hard to make out, for which the writer apologizes. He is scribbling in a shell-hole, he tells his girl, and it is filling with snow. His pencilled words run. He is a young artist and as the generals prepare for Passchendaele, he prepares his career. The snowy directions are about which London galleries she is to take his paintings, and how to hang them, and what to charge for them. For each of them the war has become a grotesque irrelevance and they don't care if the censor knows it.

I stop work to draw a Nine Lessons and Carols poster to hang in the Thatcher's – the pub at Mount Bures with the wonderful view. I hope the Church of England appreciates my skills. At the Bellringers' Dinner at the Crown I make my usual little speech of praise for the servants of the Temple, that host of choirs, organists, cleaners, embroiderers, flower arrangers, graveyard gardeners, ringers – and John, of course, to whom at Wormingford we naturally turn when there is anything we can't do. Meanwhile, feasts, Christingles, meetings and the like jostle each other more than ever they did, and there are moments when I have a sneaking envy of Parson Woodforde who, if you remember, was begged by his parishioners on Christmas Day if they might sing a carol. 'Yes, but not until I am out of the church.' Woodforde measures his communicants by the rail. 'One and a half rails this morning.' Few attend the Christmas and Easter services but his church is packed when it comes to giving thanks for a military victory, or for the recovery from sickness of a member of the Royal Family. Life at the rectory was, well, boisterous, with 'saucy' servants and prodigious meals. The Norfolk cold pierced them through and through. All the poor men of the village had dinner with him at the rectory on Christmas Day, nor over forty years did he ever take fees from the poor for their weddings, baptisms and funerals. East Anglian winters blast through his pages. On Christmas Day 1796 it was so cold he could neither eat nor sleep, and his curate 'trembled' as he took the service. Singers tended to rile him and he never understood village music. Frozen breath and frozen fingers at the west end. And carols if you were not careful.

St John of the Cross

A dawn walk along the edge of the village. The pheasants are not accustomed to this kind of thing and rise with a great clatter. But blackbirds stay put, singing the morning in with pure phrases. A low sun exposes dips in the field which would once this time of the year have presented the cold glimmer of a wintry lake in its early stages. Nothing could have been done about that, Bunyan's despondent sloughs were a fact of life. Jean's horses are browsing silhouettes on the horizon. A pair cavort and neck delicately. What privileged lives, never an hour's work, just the infatuation of girl riders to be endured once a week. They enfold me in their huge jewelled gaze as I pass. Now I can see the night being piled away in massifs of purple cloud and a raging, heatless gold sun taking over. There is a rushing noise which I know isn't a motorway. It is a grain-dryer whirling the harvest around.

We are on an escalator of parish feasts, carol services, the school concert, PCCs and meetings of every sort. News of the General Synod is supposed to trickle through. I can hear an old schoolmaster's sardonic politeness, 'Perhaps I may have the courtesy of your attention if it isn't too much bother?' I fear that our attention re synods is much distracted due to parish busyness. My complaint that I cannot be in two places at once is met with astonishment, 'Why not?' I plead work – books to write – that kind of commitment. 'Oh, you'll have plenty of time to amuse yourself once Christmas is over.' But Christmas is weeks away. Exactly, there is not a minute to spare. In Ella Leather's *The Folk-lore of Herefordshire* she mentions something called 'Tib's Eve', a day which is neither before Christmas nor after. 'They'll get that done by Tib's Eve' – meaning never.

Advent for maxims and Christmas for mottoes. Both tumble from the lectern as we read from King Solomon's Wisdom. The book speaks of us being 'born of all adventure' – as indeed God himself will be on Christmas morning. Our gift if we are wicked will be 'the waste land that smoketh', or, if we are good, the Kingdom, of course. I am touched to find in Chapter 8 Solomon confessing, 'I was a witty child and had a good spirit.' I must now brave the witty children in our primary school and read to them Eleanor Farjeon's *Mrs Malone*. Mothers will soon gather them up in cars. These country boys and girls scarcely walk a step.

Third in Advent

I imagine that we all get used to hearing some repeated epithet which sums up our circumstances, situation, house, etc. Quiet is the one which I hear most. It isn't exactly true but I know what people mean. The consolatory and healing nature of quietness pours through the scriptures. Be still, be still. I hear what, presumably, my visitors do not hear, an orchestrated sound of wind in trees, Bernard ploughing, birdsong, far cries from the sports field, water flowing, walls scratching and creaking, old clocks on their rounds, much rustling. A cult upset the Church during the seventeenth century and Quietists were thrown into noisy gaols. Establishing quiet in public worship is a gift not given to everyone. But how enchanting it can be when quiet is present. It was there the other day when I attended midday Holy Communion in Southwark cathedral, and it positively reigns in one of our local churches. Paul told the over-excited Thessalonians to 'study to be quiet'. Hearing what is going on in some Christian quarters, I decide that there are places and folk for whom a crash course on quietness wouldn't come amiss.

Matins at Wormingford. It is the day when we have to be seen as ministers and stewards of the mysteries of God. We sing imploring hymns – O come, O come, Adonais – in the grave, grey church. Afterwards, I walk over to the tall memorial to John and Christine Nash under a holly bush and see lichen blurring their names. The many Christmases with them at Bottengoms, me plucking pheasants on the doorstep, Christine preparing the goose, John playing Schubert, the cats hogging the fire, Penny and Charles's children calling to be hugged.

Fourth in Advent: St Thomas

I have been visiting the holly, now a towering barrier full of fat blackbirds. I meant to keep it within shears-bounds but it has shot to the sky. It shines and creaks. A farmer planted it generations ago, a long hedge to keep his stock from straying. He would have lopped it for boughs to razzle the great chimney and bring down the soot. Walking through crisp mud in the falling light I can just make out the marker hollies along the fields on which the ploughman drew his first furrow. This village, come to think of it, is full of holly, a most powerful plant.

As usual, preparations for the First Coming have eclipsed any sense of readiness we should have for the Second Coming, the exquisite warnings of the Advent collects notwithstanding. 'Be careful for nothing,' says Paul, but in the week before Christmas everybody is careful for everything. It is the week of the shortest day and I remember as a child how my father would announce it. 'This is the shortest day.' It must not be missed. You need what Gilbert White used to describe as 'rain, rain, dark and blowing' for a properly devastating shortest day. His entry for unseasonal Christmas days was, 'Boys play in the churchyard in their shirts.'

I shall eat, drink and be careless like the rest of the parish for tomorrow (January) we have an interregnum, which my dictionary calls a suspension of the usual ruling power. Villages in particular are deeply and curiously affected by the comings and goings of their clergy. It is an emotion worth a little study. Beyond our little world I catch the sound of diocesan plans for us cranking into action. Meanwhile, there are the journeys through the lanes to Wormingford, Little Horkesley and Mount Bures to celebrate 'The Nativity of our Lord, or the Birthday of Christ, commonly called Christmas Day'. And a present to take to Mrs Ambrose, who will be ninety on St Stephen's Day and who has worshipped nowhere else.

The Shortest Day

The shortest day and thus, by implication, the darkest week. Although, tidying the orchard, I have found myself working through sunlight into moonlight with no great inconvenience. Except to homing birds. These are full of irritation at my long-shadowed presence beneath the skeletal fruit trees and thrash irritably about in the holly hedge. Parish-wise, I have done all that can be done at this stage, typed out the Nine Lessons and Carols, persuaded Aiden to sing the first verse of 'Once in Royal David's City' solo, told Adam to read this and the patron to read that, composed special prayers for blessing seventy-five newly embroidered kneelers, painted Christmas services posters for the pub and shop, written a million letters, finished a book, skulked out of numerous festivities – one would need longer days than these to fit them in – and struggled with mammon in the supermarket.

Now I have to read. Reading has always been my way to the Way, always my way of knowing anything. I read the poet John Clare for his authoritative village sounds. One has only to open a page of him to hear every day of that Northamptonshire year, the cries, the grind, the song, the humanity, the creatures. I was reminded of him by the early darkness and the perfection of his:

> The sun had grown on lessening day
> A table large and round
> And in the distant vapours grey
> Seemed leaning on the ground.

I tell the flock about St Thomas, that so-like-us man who demanded physical proof of a spiritual reality. A week before him there was St John of the Cross, Spain's Traherne, with his daring Christian imagery, and who found that the very waiting for Christ enchanted the landscape, making the beautiful river country at Baeza distractingly lovely. For this writer scenery became the physical proof of his Lord. I have to make the most of outdoors on lessening days. The old fields know it and give their wintry best. The light is either intense or failing, nothing in between. As children, wild with excitement on black Christmas mornings, we would rush from the house to tell the goats, any stabled or passing creature what day it was. Even at this early hour the world smelled, not of incense, but of baking. Yet it seemed a different world to what had existed when we went to bed, which, when one is little, is what redemption means. Gradually, as the meal-laden hours ritually passed, it went back to its old ways.

Nine Lessons and Carols

What remains, what goes on repeating its huge sentences in my head, is the great language of the Incarnation. We put some store by our reading of it to our three congregations and are careful to hear both the words and the music. A shepherd on the radio confessed to the interviewer how much it meant to him to read the lesson. Counting nine lessons for each of our three country churches, plus all the usual ones, some forty of us must have been speaking 'Christmas' – Thanks be to God. Each one of us finding the place and reading out loud the high language of redemption. 'Don't forget Thanks be to God', I remind grown-ups and children alike, but some do forget, caught up as they are in the syntax of heaven. Boys' and girls' and old folks' voices spin through the arches, each reader releasing his consignment like a bird. Some nod friendly-like towards the altar, some don't. But afterwards, beneath the bells, I say, 'Well done! well done!' The readers are quiet, having spoken. In the beginning was the Word.

Whenever arguing with learned religious men, the Pharisees, the Temple teachers, Jesus usually enquires, 'Have you not read . . . ?' this or that scripture. But he does not ask the same question, 'Have you not read . . . ?' to prove some point with his followers. The establishment of his own literacy in that unforgettable lesson-reading scene in his home synagogue is one of those passages which makes me reread and reread. He reads Chapter 61 from Isaiah's brilliant book. Then, keeping the place with his finger, he identifies himself in the reading. This was a lesson which nobody wished to hear, the home truth which would make him homeless.

A similar excitement – the kind which bookworms share – dances about on the pages of St Augustine's *Confessions*, where that reluctant Christian describes the sing-song voice over the garden wall, a boy or girl, he can't tell which, chanting over and over again, 'Take it and read, take it and read'. The child is playing. The saint has left Paul's *Letters* unread on the games-table in the house. The child reminds him of how a friend was converted by listening to the lesson being read in church. Augustine feels guilty because he has sought salvation in some smart books 'from Athens', Paul's literary style being not quite up to what he looks for in a writer! He hurries indoors to read his own Lesson – 'Let us pass our time honourably, as by the light of day . . .' it begins. He rushes off to tell his mother. 'You can do it,' she says – or in a sentence worth reading from a lectern, 'You are powerful enough to carry out your purpose beyond all our hopes and dreams.'

Christmas

Christmas Eve. A small gift for the postmen – they have a rota – on whose endless kindnesses the logistics of this remote farmhouse turn. My towering holly hedge is snowily tipped with old man's beard but the lower boughs are a glowing mass of orange and dark green fruit and foliage. Blackbirds hustle out as I cut branches to hang over the pictures and fireplace. A ten-thirty 'midnight' at Mount Bures in order that the vicar and myself can get to an actual midnight at Wormingford. We speed through the black lanes. Among the new arts of being multi-beneficial is that of appearing to have all the time in the world when one has another church full of communicants three miles and one hour away. Most particularly at the midnight. And Mount Bures, such a sacred little temple on its military height, doesn't make this easy. It is a church to dream in. Brian plays the organ which commemorates the passing of Queen Victoria. A starved-looking John the Baptist, the parish's patronal saint, looks down at the Eucharist. Night has rubbed out the window-pictures. Joyce's new candles waver in ancient draughts. I read the Epistle and John 'In the beginning was the Word ...' After the service we stand saying happy-Christmases at the door as though we have all the time in creation. Then a scamper down Old Barn Hill, past cottages flickering with television, up Sandy Hill, by the Crown and down to St Andrew's where, mercifully, the only restiveness is in the belfry. And now, of course, the art of showing no sign that we have said and done all these great things a few minutes before. It is nearly two in the morning when Gordon drives me home where, now wide awake, I have a whisky and a read. Lights in the valley go out one by one as the congregation sleeps.

At Little Horkesley matins – crowds of families and famous singing – I preach on time and timelessness, the temporal and the eternal. I ask the children:

> And is it true? And is it true,
> This most tremendous tale of all,
>> Seen in a stained-glass window's hue,
>> A baby in an ox's stall?
> The Maker of the stars and sea
>> Become a Child on earth for me?

They think about it.

St Stephen

Savouring the darkness – few are able to indulge themselves in such a taste these pitilessly lit nights and days. I sit in the old room and watch the flames jumping across the pictures and the animals' eyes. They fire Peter Coker's 'Rendlesham', a dark wood whose finely drawn firs allow just enough space for the imagination to enter them. These black trees flourish briefly on or near the spot where King Raedwald cautiously placed a Christian and a pagan altar side by side. For half a century American bombers thundered from it; now they have flown away for good, and the natural forest darkness has reinstated itself. King Raedwald's safety-first altars have a St Thomas-like attitude, but not long after he set them up a magnificent poem, *The Dream of the Rood*, would intertwine Christianity with the ancient religion of the woodland. The Cross would become the Tree. In Kevin Crossley-Holland's translation, *The finest of trees began to talk*:

I remember the morning a long time ago
That I was felled at the edge of the forest
And severed from my roots. Strong enemies seized me
And fashioned me for their sport, bade me hold up their
    felons on high.
They shifted me on their shoulders and set me down on a hill.
It took many men to fasten me there. I saw the Lord of
    Mankind
Courageously hasten to climb upon me.
O then I dared not bend or break . . .

I take the local ramblers on the last walk of the year. It is December half-light on the Cornard hills, with now and then a faint sun and remnants of warmth. It is home ground all the way, including a long-disused stretch of Saxon lane. Shallow ditches mark parish boundaries and pollarding where axes fell centuries ago. Our feet are elephantine with clay. Our object – rambles must have an object – is to walk where Thomas Gainsborough sat to paint 'Cornard Wood'. He was young then and on the verge of things. Two or three miles to the north, more felt than seen, are the towers of All Saints and St Gregory's where his daughters were baptized. These are the little girls who chased the butterfly in the painting. We plod through slumbering apple orchards and past empty turkey sheds. The year ends. 'The last years of my life/Will be leavened with joy, for I can turn . . . to that Tree of Victory' (*The Dream of the Rood*). We cross the fields to find Workhouse Lane and so back to tea.

Suki's Mill

Suki has sent me a photograph of her mill on which is written 'Christmas morning 1891'. A man with a gun and a crow obligingly hold a pose. The miller? He and the bird are in black profile on opposite sides of the lock. There are posts for tying up the Constable family's barges. The millpool is deeply frozen and the picture is one of the deepest winter tonalities, with crystallized rushes, gauzy willows, grey ice and pure snow. The sky is colourless and, as we still say, 'with more to come'. The mill windows, handsomely Georgian, are thickly hung with floured cobwebs and there is a stack of new timber by the tow-path. Suffolk and Essex freeze twenty feet apart. If I stare long enough I will hear the cold going off like rifle shots. Here once again is the famous poetry of old plate-camera pictures, that trapped moment when the shutter falls. If the miller turned, he could just about see my farm, also frozen stiff, but the photographer won't allow that. Capturing the moment takes quite a time. The day is bitter, bitter. If the photographer doesn't put a move on, miller and crow will be as fixed as the landscape.

The mid-Advent Gospel is about a lone figure by another, warmer river with rushes which are pliant, and inviting water. And about gaping sightseers. 'What went ye out into the wilderness to see? A reed shaken with the wind? But what went ye out to see? . . . a prophet?' Such derision. What kind of person was it who went to look at, and not listen to, a prophet? Not those who would become the stewards and ministers of God's mysteries. Yet it touches me that the Christ had contemplated the Jordan reedbeds as the wind passed over them. Ours rustle as I walk from Suki's mill to Wiston church a mile or so up-stream. Somewhere beneath the grassy tumps lies the miller and his wife who, in the photograph, was beyond the view-finder and cooking the goose. I trust they attended their Saviour some time that cold Christmas of over a hundred years ago, the cameraman too. But where have all the spiders gone who spun such dusty blinds for watermills? And how do wooden buildings with their feet in torrents stay bone-dry? I rest on the churchyard seat which commemorates the organist killed in the Western Desert. A yard or two away, inside the nave, a painted ship is in full sail on the wall. I have stared as hard into this medieval picture as into any Victorian photograph.

Holy Innocents

The snow has arrived and has settled in. It came down via the coast and smells faintly of the sea. The air is so keen that I am mildly surprised when it doesn't splinter from contact with my face. Streaky blood-red dawns announced the snow and less gorgeous prophets declare there is more to come. Anxious voices ask the perennial question, 'Will I be cut off?' From civilization at the top of the track, they mean. I hope so. It is the historic prerogative of ancient farm-houses to become inaccessible now and then, and to create consternation.

Supper at Wood Hall – one of the rites of the season. The children (i.e. large young men from London) are home and there is a new dog. Chosen from hundreds at the Dogs' Home, she lies in front of the blaze stupefied by her good fortune. To be the only dog in the house! She stretches her long brindled

legs to us and the flames in turn. She may be called Bramble. When I leave she follows me across the yard, anxious not to lose a fraction of this new windfall love. It is unbelievably cold and the geese pile up on each other in their pen to make a living feather bed, the trees crack and the moon is made of ice. Two sets of fox feet imprint the top field. Where are they off to? Prayers for Lady Mallalieu, it is suggested. Countrymen – and women – continue to talk more rubbish about this creature than about any other animal. The next morning a vixen trots through the garden, nose and tail held out, and looking neither to left nor right. I stomp to the village. 'Crump' the poet John Clare's word would best describe the winter-walking sound. The church is a magnificent refrigerator and all the tombs are ice-boxes. Birds are tucking in to the berries on the holly wreaths. The view towards Bures is arctic and spectacular.

It is the Feast of the Innocents. How can a century in which elected governments have bombed, gassed and burnt millions of children deal with those two-year-olds? At the Christmas Communions I asked the worshippers not to leave the Child himself in the cold church when they drive home but to take him with them. Congregations in all three parishes were bigger than for years. True warmth and goodness existed, more than I have felt for a long time. Hackneyed carols rose to the great occasion and retreated to their original freshness. It was very beautiful. And now – the snow. And what will happen if you can't get up to the road? Nothing. That will be the bliss of it. I shall drink port and read Elizabeth Taylor, feed the wrens – and the vixen, should she call again – and have no end of a time.

New Year's Eve

The last morning of the old year. Swift saffron-and-black clouds, and motionless trees. Christmas, which took such an age to arrive, has gone in a flash. Liturgically, we have arrived at some kind of hiatus, as St Stephen, St John and the Innocents seem to go with it. The Church has no Feast of the New Year, but this is what they will expect tomorrow. And so I will do what I have always done, draw Stephen out from under the litter of Boxing Day and translate him to January 1st. This because of the only fully memorable sermon from my boyhood when a fat old bishop, long retired, stood-in for the rector and preached so marvellously on Stephen, and without notes or gesture, that I have ever after held both sight and sound of him in my head. We shall also sing Psalm 8 in which a youthful new argument silences the enemy and the avenger. The gales *en route* from Scotland will have reached Little Horkesley by then and will be roaring round the roof.

The farmers will be deep in seed catalogues distributed by my neighbour on the far side of the valley, Mr Church. Lorries filled with billions of seeds will soon be navigating the Stour lanes, taking us to the verge. I can see them from the house, those slow containers of scents and food, discreet as pregnancy. Mangle, swede, clovers of all kinds, evening primrose and borage – 'Sow in the spring at 8 kilos per acre and swath in July when seed-drop is imminent'. Ignorance of what comes up in our fields is now widespread. It reminds me of the Victorian undergraduate who, informed by an angry farmer that he was riding across corn, replied, 'I am so sorry but I am not a botanist.' The farm, still the biggest entity of most villages, has become the least seen, the least recognized aspect of rural reality. Crops nowadays are a kind of blank space between destinations, and even for those on their way to church, where they provide so much of the imagery.

The last afternoon of the old year, with the sky darkening and the wind rising. I am trudging across the wartime aerodrome. Hundreds of plovers wheel and shriek ahead. Tomorrow we shall hear of unprofitable mountains being flattened into useful fields by Isaiah's 'new sharp threshing instrument'. He would have approved these seedbeds which lay as flat as pancakes between the concrete runways. I think of Stephen and so the walk becomes a sermon-walk. The plovers think of snowstorms and so John's brassica becomes a desperate dinner interrupted by the birdscarer. Distant lights from the Glider Club suggest that, Christmas or New Year, celebration is no stickler for dates.

The last evening of the old year. Albert Camus's discovery – 'In the depth of winter, I finally learned that within me there lay an invincible summer.'

New Year's Day

Some writers break off the day's work with an unfinished sentence in order to make a kind of natural linkage in the morning. I tend to do this, not on the page but in my head. The last talk before sleep, too, often provides the subject for what I call my waking drift, a free run of interior language so powerful that it often cuts out the radio, which shouldn't be on anyway. Thus a midnight conversation about R. L. Stevenson becomes a well-developed soliloquy an hour before dawn. He is the poet of getting up, of first light and first cold. The postman is scandalized by how late village people now leave their beds; he leaves his at four. So very nearly do my commuter neighbours. It is their car headlights I see wavering through the black lanes to the station.

Few of the farms and cottages had electricity when I was a Stevensonian child, getting up at night and going to bed by day. This was the last time when light travelled inside the house, when candles and lamps moved from room to room, and, where the anti-burglar devices blaze, the stockman's storm lantern could be seen journeying round the distant byres like a will-o'-the-wisp. There has never been so much light in the world as we have now, such instant dismissals of darkness. As for half-light, gloaming, we are not allowed to know what it is. This was when we used to do our thinking. The year dies and, as they have done for centuries, parallels of yellow light from facing windows say that the valley is astir. That Light by which we are all supposed to see led Anselm to despair:

> Light, entire and inaccessible! . . .
> How far you are from me who have come so close to you.

28

To be hidden in light – how impossible! The limits of our illumination and Anselm's distress are the subjects of W. Chalmers Smith's great hymn.

The Naming of Jesus

Mild, half-lit days for the Epiphany, the manifestation of Christ beyond his own nation. Haunting music from Berlioz, and to set Peter Cornelius's chorale *Three Kings from Persian Lands Afar*. Words and tunes wind through my head as magically as they did when I was fourteen. No ordinary, commonplace representatives of the non-Jewish world would do as the first of the Lord's subjects; they had to be intellectuals – people who would be listened to when they got home. Tertullian called them 'almost kings' and one had only to set his description alongside some splendid statements in Psalm 72 – 'The kings of Tharsis and of the isles shall give presents: the kings of Arabia and Saba shall bring gifts' – and, hey presto! we have the royal Magi. Christians approved this homage from the beginning and it became one of the earliest subjects of their favourite pictures, Gaspar, Melchior and Balthazar on their knees before such a showing of the divine love. 'All kings shall fall down before him . . . and unto him shall be given the gold of Arabia; prayer shall be made unto him, and daily shall he be praised.' Psalm 72 again. The royal scene was first made manifest to me as an alabaster carving in Long Melford church. My grandmother Martha Allen had been baptized here in 1860. The Adoration of the Magi was *c.* 1360. For me as a boy these self-humbling monarchs were straight from Persian lands afar, sweet, glorious, descanted.

My grandmother told us about her confirmation in this stupendous Suffolk church – c. 1873. The Bishop of Norwich arrived in a carriage on a summer's day and was received by the rector. A thousand children, boys on the right, girls on the left, filled the nave, boys in starched collars, girls under blue veils. A marquee not much smaller than the nave billowed on the green outside. When the moment of confirmation arrived, the churchwardens carried a long plank covered with purple cloth to the Bishop and bowed. The Bishop rose, placed both hands upon the plank and the three of them walked slowly down each aisle. As the plank passed, the children bowed their heads and were confirmed. Then out they all poured to tents and tea and a silver band, manifestly members of the Church of England – and, what is more, word-perfect on its collects. All those country children gone, all those little hands touching Gaspar and Melchior and Balthazar's alabaster crowns when the rector wasn't looking, dustily folded.

Sunday After Christmas

An excursion in search of the old forest gods with the Welsh artist Glyn Morgan. He is amused when I tell him that we are driving through High Suffolk. What is elevated is my seat in his ancient Volkswagen van which gives a view of the landscape which all travellers possessed, whether riding, in carriages or on carts, or on foot, until they sank to near road level in the modern car. Glyn's van is a swaying studio, crammed with paints and turps and canvases. Rare sunshine clarifies the most distant objects and blazes across the winter wheat. The homesteads which the farmers abandoned for Massachusetts during the 1630s stare comfortably at each other through the leafless trees. Grandfather's parlour is full of GATT talk. I take Glyn to see the grand forest god in the Bull at Long Melford, a branch in one hand, a swan in the other, and his head crowned with oak leaves. He was carved about 1450. A decoration or a shrine?

The confidences of pain. How does one reply when the language of comfort has dwindled into the stock answer? I find that I often possess an intuitive knowledge of who is ill in this countryside, and certainly of those who find not being well interesting. The latter are far less keen on getting better than on being heard. Others, suddenly struck down by the announcement of disease, have little to say. I listen to their silences, their fright.

Twelfth Night

Twelfth night. The holly has been taken down and burnt near the little waste by the marsh, the temperature has soared and the ponds have melted. Nor is there an ounce of wind. The Epiphany edition of *The Times Literary Supplement* has arrived and is devoted to War. Its cover-picture of John Nash's 'Over the Top' stares up among the Christmas cards. At first it reminds me of his love-affair with snow, of how he would telephone around to find out whether any of the neighbours were as cut-off as he was. 'We are *impassable*' – triumphantly. I would shovel paths for his wife, for their cats, for an intrepid caller, and above me the huge oaks would groan because of the extra loads they had to carry. John stayed indoors, painting snowscapes through the windows and using the glazing bars for measurements. Now here, come home to roost, as it were, is his first big snow, painted in a Buckinghamshire seedshed in 1918 after he had been rescued from the Western Front. He and his brother Paul, who worked by his side, were paid thirty shillings a day by the government for their 'official' war pictures. He told me that the commission enquired if he would like to return to the Somme to 'refresh his memory'. I suspect that they would have received his famous glacial glance.

The soldiers going over the top are in the Artists' Rifles. The fighting apart, it is a battle to get out of the frozen trench in their thick uniforms. Impeded, they plunge and crunch to their annihilation. One of them, said John, has been given the face of a musician he had heard singing Schubert lieder at a Queen's Hall concert – 'I put him in because everything good was going, you know.' He had also married a half-German girl in 1918. She would sing Schubert into her eighties.

The Magi are blest with some splendid songs and poetry. What trio named Gaspar, Melchior and Balthazar would not have been? Their story is a perfect one, being both factual and mysteriously iridescent. When I was a child it got mixed up with the Arabian Nights. A friend brought me small phials of myrrh and frankincense for Christmas, just one drop of either on the hot stove filled the house with a rich and moody scent. And sumptuous remains the language of Epiphany – that word itself, as well as 'orient' and that describing of the three brilliant travellers on their knees before their 'star'. The ancient responses which followed the Epiphany processional took Christ out of the firmament and made Him oceanic:

> The voice of the Lord is upon the waters.
> The Lord is upon many waters.

The Plague

And so 'the Christmas' comes down, the withered holly, the tipsy cards. The rooms look Spartan and in need of flowers. The fridge is filled with the crumbs of feasts and packets which say 'Best until December 25th'. Last week icy trinkets, released by the morning sunshine, fell to the earth with the sound of Eastern music, and winds from Duncan's fields cut your head off. This week it is Jane Austen's favourite weather – muggy. I love it too and would have gardened had it not been for the plague. Half the village has been laid low with it and we vie with each other on the telephone concerning our sufferings. Mine have been more disgusting than agonizing and had I been able to speak I would have had to play them down for decency's sake. As it was, my croakings eloquently expressed the superior nature of my flu, and I was able to enjoy universal concern. But how nasty this disease is. One feels that one should go about with a bell shouting, 'Unclean! Unclean!' Max has been heroic, sitting on me with cold wet feet from the grass, indifferent to catching anything worse than mice and rumbling with immortality. It is most encouraging. All he asks is four round meals a day and a stove which never goes out. It is little enough.

I try to work but flu says cut it out. It says, 'I have un-stopped all the avenues of ill, and this means that you are going to be half-witted for the next few days, so make the most of it. It is ridiculous your trying to review Titus Burckhardt's *Chartres*. Such glories need a clear head and yours is like an old flock bed with a sewer running through it. Try something within your mental reach.' I try *The Wind in the Willows*. I see that it was presented to Christine in 1916 by Eleanor and Bruce, and that long ago it met with an accident, for it is heavily water-stained. Flu says, 'Never mind if you can't understand it all as you aren't too bright.' A little Horkesley specialist advises on how to make a whisky toddy, a sickly hot beverage, but all that it does is to evoke echoes (or spasms) of an ancient invalidism, like shawls and faltering steps. Flu says, 'Thou fool. Not even the combined recipes of the Medical Research Council are going to help. I am not to be fought, I am to be endured. Surrender to me. Give up letters, socializings, anything remotely intelligent. Mr Toad is an Einstein compared with you at this moment.' What a novelty – to be quasi dumb and delicate. Were the glass-makers of Chartres laid low with le flu – just now and then? Poor creatures on that dank plain.

Epiphany

New-year's week is as good a time as any for field-edge walking if you can stand the mud. There is much to see which will not be visible in summer. For one thing the old year's last flowers, and spring breaking cover. I walk where a community settled long ago in what looks like an open-cast flint mine. It is our first village, made during prehistory in an elbow of land by the river. There are millions of stones among which will be an axe, an arrow, something once useful. A young neighbour with keener eyes has picked up dozens of both. John's corn grows where these ancients sowed their emmer-wheat. How unreachable they are, even with a sharpened flint in my hand. This is immemorial, flint country where the church towers shine with crystallized quartz harvested from the soil, and where I persist in the vain hope some splinter will say more than such fragments tend to do about a world where there was no writing, thus no 'history'.

Paul, like John, like so many of us, struggled hard to compre-hend the 'beginning'. In the Epiphany epistle, in exquisite language, Paul insists that 'the unsearchable riches of Christ' have been 'hidden in God' from the beginning but now there is nothing to prevent them from being shown to all men at all times. This village's beginnings are lost in flint. Historians have found its farming, I try to find its voices, talking, singing, cursing, maybe, when the stone splits the wrong way. At the carol service my lesson was Isaiah 5 in which the land is freed of stones to make the Beloved's vineyard and the hooves of the horses of those who herald him 'shall be counted like flint' (hard, obdurate). The English translators knew their flints. 'When Israel went out of Egypt', says the psalmist in that happy hymn, the Lord turned flint into a fountain.

I plod back home. Many thousands of rooks have taken over the white sky. They soar haphazardly like carbonized newsprint from the bonfire, each black fleck of bird on its wind current, soundless, blissful. I have to sit on the wet bank to watch them. They spiral and climb until they are little more than rook-dust and not a caw to say what they are up to.

Epiphany One

A repeated journey adds up to a form of autobiography. Going over the same ground, if only once or twice a year, claims it for oneself. Although my life has recently alternated between some of the longest and briefest of travels – to Sydney, to the village – trips to London since childhood now mount to a sizeable private chapter.

So here I am on a fair morning with the commuters, looking out while they are looking down *en route* to Southwark, that great setting-out spot and site of prisons and releases. Personal references slide past the window. Witham and Dorothy Sayers, and my youthful self chairing the lecture she was giving on the Emperor Constantine. Then a huge house from which the first Prince Charles and the Marquis of Buckingham, wearing false beards and calling themselves John and Tom Smith, rode away to fetch home the Infanta. Then platforms whose architecture I know by heart but on which I have never trod. Then the vast marble litter of Manor Park Cemetery where the proto-commuters sleep, and then Liverpool Street Station itself, gloriously dreadful for most of my days, now a palace. I wonder at my fellow-travellers; if they don't soon look out at what is passing there will be a big gap in their recollections.

I wait for the wood of what I suppose must be Harold Wood, an exquisite track-side forest in which I have never caught anyone walking. But all the way there leaps along that wayward wilderness of plants which my old friend Richard Mabey calls the unofficial countryside from which there should be E. Nesbit children waving, but from where there is a rampant flourish of blackthorn and sudden flights of birds. I am reading The Acts of the Apostles, Luke's brilliant travel-book in which it is said the sacred and the profane meet on common ground.

How they all got about! The journey was the almost impossible theological one from Jerusalem to Rome, yet they made it. I return in the dark to the old house, and with all the associations on the way blacked out. Trains, so pleasant for me in the light, become tragic when they cut through the night. The commuters rock, their eyes shut, their papers slipping, and if they are telling me anything it is that we are all in the same boat.

St Benedict the Librarian

Two walks into the light, one at dawn, the other in the early evening. Whilst trudging to the School Governors' meeting during the latter, I am made suddenly aware that the village is almost as lit up as the town, what with old gas-lamps rescued, electrified and planted in front gardens, and the nerve-racking blaze of security lights which makes the passing of some friends' houses reminiscent of an escape from a gulag. The modest bulb illuminating the vine (mostly) of my old house having fused, I am extra conscious of all this rustic brilliance. One of the ways in which the world is divided is by those who replace broken things at once, and those who do not. For a week or more I have had to feel my way through the garden, taking extra care not to meet the yucca. The lane to the school is full of fog. Vision is reduced to uncurtained windows jumpy with television. Then comes our church, apparently all lit, though why? Thousands of glassy fragments sparkle in its traceries. They seem to swim in the river mist, contract, shift, shine. All this light – and from one tiny, wavering-in-the-draught spark above the Reserved Sacrament. It plays over Arthur's fresh grave in the liveliest fashion.

The dawn walk was to the rickety garage to collect the post and the paper. This about 8.30 under dripping trees. Moles were having a field-day in the orchard, which is the best place for it. I find this stroll notorious for its importuning tasks. Clearing beds of old sticks, raking the ditch, weeding, tidying – and of course fitting a new outside light. The post is full of invitations to give talks. Life could be a seminar. Today is 17 January 1996 and the *Independent*, even in this white gloom, seems to have turned into a sheet of Christmas-wrapping, very spangled and pretty. Indoors, it reveals itself – manifests itself, to be exact. For here on the front page is the universe at the moment of its creation, caught by the Hubble Space Telescope. At first glance the picture has the suffused splendour of great glass such as Chartres. Then the information begins to flow through it, and it is awesome. I read on. Delegates at the meeting of the American Astronomical Society were so overwhelmed by what they were seeing that their usual scientific language forsook them. Confessing 'wonderment', they were momentarily at one with the Magi. The statistics of this photograph added up to 'In the Beginning' – and these only of an area no larger than a grain of sand in the region of the Great Bear. Just a speck of time and space, just a glimmer of all the light there is, just billions of stars.

Epiphany Two

How glad one is to discover an artefact from childhood reprieved by time, or in this case the town council. It is a public fountain with two dog-troughs and a great chained bronze cup for parched boys. I used to read the carved inscription 'Whosoever drinketh this water shall thirst again' with bewilderment. Obviously. My great-uncle's pony may have swigged here when he went to market. Modern traffic now swirls around this charitable water-hole, which is dry. Not so the surrounding countryside. Cornfields look like paddy-fields and trees stand in lakes. The many old 'water lanes' are avoided, for they are truly awash. I have diverted the ochre stream which is my track to the main ditch, where it roars. It was weather like this which washed England's agriculture away during the late nineteenth century; a terrible disaster.

The minor prophets rage during the Epiphany. Amos, claiming that he was nothing more than a dresser of sycamore figs (i.e. an ordinary countryman) proves himself to be, on the contrary, a major poet of denunciation. The Epiphany touches me deeply, as it must all star-gazers. I am ravished by Peter Cornelius's *Three Kings from Persian Lands Afar*, which is to be taken 'rather slowly' to match the gait of the camels in the waddies, I presume.

We have laid Gerry, prisoner-of-war, tree-feller, church-warden, in his grave. The indigenous people make their full statement on such an occasion and there is not much room in the church for those of us who have only been here for twenty years. The sun blazes on the floods and the earth from Gerry's tomb looks warm and friable, and I find myself taking a botanical interest in it as the coffin goes down. The sward here is famous for its harebells. A blue land under the old motte it will be when the winter has gone. Historically, the registers show a great clearance during the Epiphany. It was Heaven to those who could never stop working. The River Colne glitters like knives in the drenched pasture.

Epiphany Three: Conversion of St Paul

The east wind doth blow and it is no time for meres and marshes, but as host to a naturalist there can be no hugging the fire. This is the wind which they say locally 'doesn't bother to go round you' and which no anorak can cheat. Our normally placid village mere rocks violently and a dull roar has set itself up where, soon, the swans will gleam and breed. Richard Mabey and I move on to the Alde, which can be two-jersey country in June, for me the loveliest of all wetlands, with its Japanese economy of view. Mother Julian called the coast 'the seaground' but the eccentric behaviour of the Alde insists that wherever we look is river-ground. Here, meteorologically speaking, the wind cuts our heads off. To compensate there are a million tossing reed plumes, miles of plants transformed into a purple-grey ocean by the gale. We struggle to Iken through its howling music and make a dash for the church like sanctuary-seekers, recover our breath and listen to the tempest thumping its nave. It is where St Botolph, 'a man of remarkable life and learning', is said to have lived during the seventh century. East Anglians were very fond of him and took care that a church dedicated to him stood immediately inside the gate of the towns they had to visit. A reed saint. And with what the Reverend Sidney Smith called 'good fires', one hopes.

We walk in Iken wood among the ancient oaks, comforted by the evidence of so much fuel at hand for the saint. It is warmer here than in the church, only just below zero and quite cosy. Sexagesima approaches when St Paul admits being a fool for Christ. What a familiar wilderness all this is; I am positively on nodding terms with Botolph. 'What went ye out into the wilderness to see?' demanded the Lord scornfully. 'A reed shaken by the wind? You went to *see* a prophet!' Prophets are not for staring at but for listening to. John was a sensational sight down by the reed-beds of the Jordan. It would have been a reed from those wetlands which reached up to the parched lips on Calvary.

I tell Richard about the peach orchards of Iken. I am pleased with its enormous pig farm, free-range, with little Nissen-hut sties for grunting couples. They say that pigs can see the wind.

Timothy and Titus

Until this week the year has been like some old vehicle lurking darkly in a barn which shows signs of life but won't actually start up and emerge. Admittedly there was the pretty snow, although a general grimness of the atmosphere seemed to drain its vitality. Then, unbelievably, the sun was warm on the study window and outside the world could be seen getting going. Gordon then arrived with our parish magazine for

February – the 339th issue and renamed *The Worm* – and I take it from him with disbelief. Who has wrought this wondrous change? Not, I must hastily add, that anything can detract from the dedicated toil which went into producing the previous 338 copies. But this *Worm* with its banner inspired by the window celebrating our version of the St George and the Dragon legend, and its polished format, and all the sacred and secular news you need to know so handsomely set out, whose work is this? That of David and Charles, of course, for whom layout, keyboards, type and editing have no mystery. Michael the Vicar writes coolly about the Lottery, taking his text from Vespasian – 'Money has no smell' – and Sylvia in a poem listing our celebrities puts me with Elizabeth I, who came this way in 1562.

Parish magazines can be divisive, having everything to say to those within church culture and making the rest of the community feel out of things. They can still include items and styles which would not be tolerated in any other publication. A part of me is not offended by this as I wander in and out of ancient buildings to look at their treasures and delights – countless of them around here – ending up in the back pew to scan the local services, the flower rota (intriguing names), moved by the priest's revealing monthly letter, and filled with understanding for the little book, having myself written so many of them. Yet the 339th issue of our 'Newsletter', as it is called, emphasizes what I have always felt, which is that a parish magazine should be intelligent, unapologetically 'spiritual' as well as the first place you would look to find out what is going on. It should be good.

I will not be showing off my Early English to tell the village that the 'Worm' of Wormingford is Widemonde in the Domesday Book – young Widermund who lived by the ford no doubt. Who would exchange him for a dragon with a girl in its jaws? See our north aisle window, *c*. 1920. David and

Charles will be devouring copy for March. They could be evangelists unawares.

Jean's horses run on the hillside in praise of February, chasing and wheeling in the afternoon light, their manes flung out like flags.

Fifty Years After Auschwitz: 26 January 1995

The week has been partly dominated by images of closed trucks carting baby animals to ports and humanity to ovens, and by the unexpected radiance, if you like, of the commissioning service of our new bishop. I say unexpected in the sense that it soared away from the conventions which necessarily must surround such an occasion. But first the wormwood of Auschwitz. Fifty years have only served to intensify it and, as film footage of those unspeakable rail journeys runs across our little screens, I, like everyone else, stare with incredulity. If we were only seeing this one-off black and white horror born of a one-off criminal politics, it would be horror beyond anything previously imaginable, but we – I am sitting in the warm room with a friend watching the trucks – know that the 'final solution' is that to a problem which had wickedly preoccupied Christian Europe for centuries. It is strange to remember – to be unable to forget – that most of those who operated this dreadful business had been baptized. Not only were the trucks in motion, but all kinds of thinking. And so it will be, not for fifty years but for always. I thought of, had things been different, trucks being filled in some siding at King's Cross and of many thousands of East End children.

The poet Sidney Keyes, who died 'from unknown causes while in enemy hands' whilst fighting in the Western Desert, wrote:

> Never a day, never a day passes
> But I remember them, their stoneblind faces
> Beaten by arclights, their eyes turned inward
> Seeking an answer and their passage homeward:
>
> For being citizens of time, they never
> Would learn the body's nationality.

The day before the Auschwitz half-centenary we went to Colchester to welcome Edward Holland, previously the Pauline-sounding Bishop in Europe, now Edward Colchester. As I said, all the civic trappings were present, all the diocesan state. But so too was something fresh and enchanting. Perhaps it was due to having trumpet voluntaries between each verse of the Epiphany hymns, slowing us up and causing the singing to become unfamiliarly sumptuous, or because everything was good and true and, being Anglican, faultlessly entered into. It was the Conversion of St Paul. We were in St Botolph's. This East Anglian saint's churches were built near the entrances of cities so that Suffolk and Norfolk people could meet someone who would understand them when they left home.

Epiphany Four

A child musing on the blessed ignorance of gulls as they wing low over the field – 'They don't know it's Wormingford.' His friend – 'They don't know it's Thursday!' The village's verdict on some fortunate neighbour – 'He doesn't know he's born.' The poet Gray had no doubts that ignorance was bliss. He was thinking of young Etonians. Is the Lord's wrath against those who 'offend one of these little ones' an attack on the clever who have the means to shake or destroy a simple faith? I have always thought so.

It is the School Governors' meeting and we are condemned to Little Ease as we are taken through the DoE's Financial Regulations and Scheme of Delegation by patient Mr Critchley. I have walked all the way through the night lanes and a fine rain. First along the track, still squelchy after the hunt sploshed down it on Boxing Day, then along the main road, then across the playing-field still liquid after football, then down by the church where the great painted windows hang gold-black in their traceries. No moon or stars but stubby catkins make promising patterns against the featureless sky. I am late. They have drunk all the tea but remain subdued by the enormity of the agenda. I take my place at the bottom of the class alongside Betty, who is scribbling in a minute notebook with a gold pencil – probably some imploring verse from a metrical psalm. The churchwarden and the organist, both extremely clever, are way up the table and too far away to cheat from. At least it's cheering to be grown-up. Mr Critchley can hardly throw a book at us. He is tolerant, knowing that we are only farmers and innkeepers and authors, etc. and can scarcely be expected to grasp such matters as 'All virements are to be recorded by means of form BH8, see appendix A, sequentially numbered.' All I can think

of is Henry Reed's *The Naming of Parts*, that masterpiece on inattention. What was the Diocesan Education Committee thinking about when it appointed me its representative? How I wish I was in the morning playground having a lesson on the rain-gauge. The headmaster is considerate and doesn't halt the proceedings to shout, 'That man there, tell us in your own words what we have been talking about!' Maybe we shall come to the school library, and then I can show off. Vast sums are being mentioned. All this for St Andrew's Church of England (Aided) Primary School (23 pupils)? Gradually, like the top water on the fields, it all sinks in. Our responsibility – our power!

All round the room the Vikings are coming in lovely Alfred Wallis ships. Across the cobalt North Sea they sail, all oblong canvas and ferocity. They are just off Felixstowe – our pupils are stunning artists. Their raiders will soon be putting the MoE to the sword. I wish I could see what Betty is writing – her resignation? I put down the date of the next meeting – which is next week!

The Presentation of Christ in the Temple

An extraordinary week of birdsong to accompany the Presentation of Christ in the Temple, not only here but throughout the land, apparently. Such torrents of bird-music in the late afternoons. A chance confession by Meriel made me think of animism as well as these worshipful sounds. This was that as a child she had laid secret claim to a flint in the school wall. She suddenly remembered it, 'my stone', and there true enough it was, propping up Alma Mater as it had done since 1871, purple-black and capable. She touched it lovingly.

The little gesture reminded me of the private realm of children's animism, with its magic trees and posts and indeed in my own case a fat dark cobble set in a brick courtyard which I talked to when I was six.

The stoniness of things is revealed by the recent rains. They have washed away the thin veneer of dirt and plants from green lanes and there, a scrubbed mosaic, shine the millions of flints which many generations of country children carried from the fields to mend the parish roads. The sarsens, or stranger-stones – the non-indigenous rocks which slid from Scotland to our parts during the ice-age – which I carried into the garden from where the ploughmen piled them long ago, are also looking their best. The Indian writer Prafulla Mohanti regarded them gravely. 'My village (Nanpur, Orissa) has a new god; it is a stone.' I thought of Jacob's sacred feeling for his stone at Bethel and of how he asked his brothers to gather stones, and of how he and Laban declared 'Mizpah' on this cairn – the beautiful 'the Lord watch between me and thee when we are absent one from another.' Mizpah used to be written in semi-precious stones on mothers' brooches.

East Anglians have always been torn between accepting their 'everlasting flint' (*Romeo and Juliet*) as a blessing or as a curse. Flint has been our unavoidable catch-crop. Silicon has been our never-failing harvest. It provided great treats when we were small. Gloriously blessed was the child who had a stone-pit at hand, and few of us did not. How many hammers were lost in them only fathers knew as we cracked open the more promising flints to find the toads which, as everyone knew, lived in them. We were also beguiled by 'dawn stones', or stones from In the Beginning. Plenty of those, too, needless to say. We did now and then find a fossil. The trouble was our fantasy and our heresy. 'Go and play in the stone-pit.' Play! Never were we more serious. Overhead we could hear the screech of the share on more flints and the thump of hooves, and a kind of half-whistled song. 'What are you boys doing down there?' What the ploughman did when he was our age.

Septuagesima

'Noises off', though more Ayckbourn than Shakespeare. A fearful comedy along the Suffolk border. 'How quiet it is!' say visitors to the old farm in the fold of land. They mean that I cannot hear the traffic, not that I am deaf to what is going on. How could I be these news-infested days? It was ever so, but in other circumstances. Bunyan from his cell heard a trumpeter blare curfew as the Ouse bridge was closed (it would sound for Mr Valiant-for-Truth on the *other* side); Julian from her cell heard the continuous rumble of the world as it entered Norwich via the Wensum. Just how much one should know by way of the News, or how little, is a religious question. A friend has just given his television set to a surprised caller. Is he a candidate for the calendar or for the social services? He has turned the newscasters out, lock, stock and goodbye smiles, and is master in his own house. We should try it. It is a lay form of Trappism.

A sudden exultation in the climate has brought me to the boggy ground to where primulas, marsh marigolds (said to have been stolen from a Vatican lake in the nineteenth century) and the dreaded Japanese knotweed are asking to be freed from last year's debris. As a devout member of the Mirabel Osler sect – *A Gentle Plea for Chaos* – I allow the garden its beautiful muddles. It is at this moment that I hear the spring as 'noises off' in the sounds of a different wind, a louder blackbird, a less threatening stream. Silence being a too-advanced state of noiselessness for someone like me, I settle for quiet. 'How quiet it is!' can be said in cities, or should be sometimes, and unnaturally so where they have been pedestrianized. Crowds walking through central Ipswich with a sound like blown leaves. The quietness of streets in which children no longer play, the hermetic quiet of the double-glazed room. 'How quiet it is!' I tell myself when I am away from home, missing what those who come to see me cannot hear.

Caedmon

Snow-bound. The last time it happened an American friend asked if I knew John Greenleaf Whittier's poem *Snow-bound?* This was a few years back. It is one of the great snow poems and, rereading it after discovering the track up to the lane blocked by drifts, I was struck by Whittier's 'hereditary' memory of English winters. He is a boy cooped up with his family and a handful of neighbours in a clapboarded farmhouse in Haverhill, Massachusetts, but subconsciously his experience is still that of Haverhill, Suffolk. The same – marvellously described – north wind, an identical interior. And the same just Quaker God, of course. The rattle and roar, and the vast white silences are made to contain, as it were, the noble domestic life. Blizzards are among literature's chief devices for casting together strange bedfellows, and this one is no exception, for among the neighbours is Lady Hester Stanhope's equally eccentric friend Miss Livermore. The pair of them had fallen out on the question of which one of them took precedence at the Second Coming to ride into Jerusalem with the Lord. *Snow-bound* offers a lad's view of religious fantasy and rationality having to exist in the closest proximity until the thaw. Anyway, sans the media, what has humanity ever done in captivity but tell its own tales? These, though enchanting, come second best to the tale of the snow itself. It is the same tale it always tells, first in a wild rage, then so quietly that you can hear the flakes crystallizing the trees.

On Ash Wednesday I made a reconnaissance to see if I could get to church to read Joel's fierce demands – 'Blow the trumpet in Zion, sanctify a fast, call a solemn assembly, gather the people ... let the priests, the ministers of the Lord, weep between the porch and the altar' – but found I had to climb Duncan's steep field if I was not to vanish in drifts. These were combed by the wind into rising segments like the roof of the Sydney Opera House and impassable. There was a pale new moon as sharp as a sliver of ice and air which spoke daggers. So home to a little Lenten music and an apology to Joel for being so effete. The worst thing is that many of the village people live on gritted roads and my snow-bound descriptions are put down to writer's hyperbole. It took an ox-team to 'break the drifted highways out' in Whittier's poem, and should the worst come to the worst (which it never does) I dare say Duncan will send a tractor down. But not yet. Also by the time that these luxuriating thoughts on inaccessibility are read, the drifts will be streams hurrying to the river, and the way will be clear.

St Valentine

For the rain it raineth every day. Absurdly, I find myself, nose to pane, staring through sliding globules at the drenched exterior. I am a child again and the worst words in the world are being said: '*No*, you cannot go out.' Neither could the farm labourers, as they were still called. They watched their tiny wages being washed away. Those who could had put a few bob by for a rainy day. So much of the rural background of the Gospels needed no explanation to the worshipping country people of only fifty years ago. The Septuagesima epistle is all about labourers' wages and its stark equalizing and bleak conclusion would have caused some flinching in the pews. A penny if you toiled a full day, a penny if you toiled an hour. Farmer neighbours splosh in. Having been properly trained by their wives, they kick off their wellingtons to reveal neat little liners over their socks in which they can pad around like Muslims. Outside, the field-drains are singing and with a good ear on a pouring morning it is possible to pick up all the cascading water music of the February land. In the city the damp white faces of the homeless glimmer in the under-passes.

St Valentine has come and gone. Poor martyr, how we take his name in vain. He had nothing to do with sweethearts. It was just that his feast coincides with the day on which the spring birds mate – 14 February. Little is known of him. The public mating on the Valentine pages of the newspapers makes gruesome reading, and for the press a nice annual earner. At least Margery Brews, writing to her 'Voluntyn' in 1477, kept it private: 'Myn herte me byddes ever more to love yowe truly over all erthely thing.' It was on a drear Sunday afternoon in February that the girl-farmer Bathsheba in Hardy's *Far from the Madding Crowd* amuses herself by sending the most tragic valentine in English literature. It breaks the heart of its recipient, Farmer Boldwood. It says, 'Marry me' – but it is a joke. To decide whether she will send it to a boy or to this ageing man, Bathsheba throws a hymnbook in the air – shut, Boldwood, open, Teddy. 'Of love as a spectacle Bathsheba had a fair knowledge; but of love subjectively she knew nothing.'

On Septuagesima I preach on God making something out of nothing. There was a void and he filled it. There was darkness and he lit it. This is what creation means. Below us, the Stour streams to the sea. Beside us the much rained-on tombs make clear reading. Some of their inscriptions are real valentines.

Sexagesima

My old friend from up top has walked in to see me. He was ninety-five last Michaelmas. In church he sits in what he calls 'farmers' pew'. He talks about his native Ayrshire which he left as a small boy in one of those Abrahamic migrations to fresh pasture when the Scottish crofters came to East Anglia. There is an obelisk to his Covenanter ancestor in the deserted home fields, a poor young man shot by Claverhouse in front of his wife and children. This friend is one of a substantial group of ancient worshippers whose prayer impresses me. There they are, in the various naves, all kneeling, some bonily like stick insects, some mightily like tumbled oaks, their snowy heads low, at prayer. What is their 'dream', I wonder – 'A dream cometh through the multitude of Business' says that pessimistic poet we call the Preacher. The business to which he refers is divine worship and his is the only reference I know of in scripture to those insights and imaginings which liturgy creates. Upright, and scarcely bothering to glance at their books, they sing two perfectly articulated dreams which came through the multitude of business known as the service, Benedictus and Nunc Dimittis, in the form of farewell songs by two good old men.

The old don't like to be hurried away after the service. They want to huddle and chat and beam and 'belong'. My dreams take a sociological turn and I think, looking at the aged women, there go the last of the gleaners, and the last of those who rang for tea. 'I've been a bad lot, my dear,' says Mary, with everything about her saying something quite different. 'I'm pleased to hear it,' I answer. It is our standard repartee. Embracing her is like enfolding a warm mountain. She is older than Anna, who was eighty-four and 'who talked about the Child'. 'Eighty – why that's nothing these days!' But it is, and they know it. They know it by their prayer. Collectively, it seems to go before our own with its deserved and simple precedence. 'I could tell you things', says Mary, 'but I can't find the words.' George Herbert was only thirty-nine when he found words to say, 'The day is spent and hath his will on me:/I and the sun have run our races.'

Quinquagesima

Blissfully warm, the sky filled with a double range of clouds, the higher ones static, those beneath moving across them in a fast drift. It is one of those sepia days so special to these islands and often so wrongly written off as dull. Matins at Little Horkesley, where another kind of drift lightens the tombs. Spring grasses. I preach on St Paul's acknowledgement of the variety of human experience. This is the day, I discover, on which he requires us, of all things, to be affectionate to one another and to love without dissimulation. He should glimpse, two millenniums later, the Sunday newspapers spread out among the vegetables in our farm shop, eye-catching, like beetle-wings on dung. After lunch I plod about the orchard cutting elder, my head working overtime on a novel I am writing.

Water-testing time when Ian, the Environmental Health Department man, arrives to sample the stream. I am one of over a hundred householders who live where no mains flow. The farm water makes an adventurous progress from a tiny spring to a tank in the old roof via ditches and brick cisterns, and visitors have to be taught how to respect it. What I don't use rushes off to the river. The ditches are lined with ivy, campion and hartstongue brought from Cornwall. I display these wonders to Ian, not to mention the wonder of not having to pay water-rates, but he takes small bottlefuls away with him, rather like a pilgrim to Walsingham, except, I'm afraid, my much-loved supply isn't a bit holy to him. I was born drinking from a well and I expect I shall die drinking from a stream, but there will have been a fair stretch of living in between. And what a blessing to have forgotten elementary chemistry. Not so for Ian the tester.

How aware one is of cadence in worship, of a descending language which says things as perfectly as they can be said. For oneself, that is. I am aware of my own voice in church being cadent with those English Christian writings and music which have fallen to me over the years and which, because of my age, cannot now be replaced by a latter cadence, however in tune with the times. I hear this old, mighty language just as Theodore Roethke went on hearing that which influenced him – 'I take this cadence from a man named Yeats.' When the other day we sang 'O my Saviour Lifted' it was not only the cadence of a Victorian bishop which filled a country church, but also that longing for God which tumbles down to us from age to age, and which outdates all dates.

Ash Wednesday

Ash Wednesday, Ramadan too. Searching for the vestry key in the dark I pile my robes on John Constable's uncle Abram's tomb. Stanley our priest-in-charge refrains from weeping between the porch and the altar but walks behind us singing a bitter little hymn by John Monsell. The austerities of Lent seem to suit old Suffolk types like me and the mysterious chill which appears to have got trapped in our sanctuary since the Middle Ages says, 'Welcome'. Cold damask, cool language, no Gloria. Welcome to the desert.

Another kind of starvation is feeding through faster than we thought it could, and has to be mentioned if we are not to be accused of living in some kind of rustic nowhere. In brief, that threatened by the financial disaster into which the Church has been plunged. The effect on countless village parishes which have so scrupulously paid their way is rather similar to that of respectable Victorian families caught up in a stock-bank crash. Our congregations contain, as well as those who can easily afford greater giving, many dear Christians who are relicts of the traditional farmworkers' poverty, or who toil in local factories and shops with little security. These givers are stunned by the Commissioners' losses.

Now and then I try out some economic fancifulness on one of our bishops; they are kind to me and indulge my poetic notions. Might not the day come when a holy young man (or woman) would arrive in a community such as Wormingford, say, and make a bargain with it? 'I will be your priest-without-money if you will give me a small warm house, some food, a bike and a subscription to the London Library, and if you won't turn me out in the direction of the Sunshine Home when I am eighty, for the senescence of godly men has a sacred wonder all its own.' The bishop to whom I said this smiled.

A flower garden might be added. I walk in my Lenten garden before breakfast. Thousands of flowers are out. Newly married mallards fly out of the horse-ponds, showering the willow. The new digging fills me with pride. These eight a.m. strolls provide a balance to the cynicism which, in the light (or dark) of so much of what occurs these days, might well spoil what I so naturally feel about the Faith.

Ash Wednesday – T. S. ELIOT

'Ash Wednesday – already!' says the old choir-leader, when I give her the hymns. 'The year races. When I was a girl a week took its time.' The three parishes will be together at Little Horkesley in the church which rose from the ashes of an air raid and I shall kneel on the fractured tomb of a gentleman who died in the spring of 1666. His arms show a dove with 'an olive leaf pluckt off'. On Saturday I shall lay dear Micky's ashes in the rain-soft earth by the wall. How efficiently and swiftly we 'come to dust' in the late twentieth century. How the symbols of violence and peace pace our history. I shall read from Joel, a favourite author of mine – his magnificent, 'Blow the trumpet in Zion, sanctify a fast, call a solemn assembly, gather the people . . .'

Reading T. S. Eliot's *Ash Wednesday*, I am reminded of Barbara Pym sending me fragments of her delightful diary on postcards from her hospital bed. She said that her church's chief claim to fame was that Eliot was received into the Church of England there on 29 June 1927. Finstock, Oxfordshire. It was there that she worshipped, devoutly and amusedly, in what one visitor had called 'a tattered hamlet'. It was there that T. S. Eliot came for baptism. And it is in such unprepossessing spots up and down the land that the Faith takes root, the Faith which flowers everlastingly in poetry and philosophy, in historic association and private discovery. The Gospel for Ash Wednesday contradicts Joel's orders. Do not parade your ashes. Fast in secret. And remember that the moth and rust must eventually reduce all that you physically possess to dust. A dancing dust, judging by the motes caught in the early March sun which streams through my room.

Eliot published his *Ash Wednesday* in 1930 all unknowingly

at the beginning of a decade in which a politics would consign the Lord's own nation to the ash-pit. Lenten imagery from the grim Commination service and the Bible flickers through it. 'Turn thou us, O good Lord, and so shall we be turned' the congregation begs at the end of the Commination. The poet says:

> Because I do not hope to turn again
> Let these words answer
> For what is done, not to be done again
> May the judgement not be too heavy upon us.

After Ash Wednesday come the weekly house-communions at the farms, the (let us hope) drying-up of the sodden fields, the pencil greening of the willows, the nesting of the birds. Nothing dusty. Indeed, the opposite. In the poem the birds sing, 'Redeem the time, redeem the dream.'

The Green Man

Snow has an endearing way of hanging about long after the conditions which caused it have fled before higher temperatures. As boys we would find some gully or green lane still piled high with it when the rest of the village was in another climate. It persisted on the steep banks as we entered Hadleigh and I was suddenly reminded of a childish hopefulness bordering on conviction that, given a little encouragement, it would lie there all through the summer. I was in Hadleigh to write about the Green Man paintings of an artist friend, an

entire gallery of them. This powerful and persisting intelligence
had been slandered in our youth as a Wild Man or Woodwoser,
a miserable survivor of paganism whose lowly duty it was to
support the font. Four Wild Men and four lions balanced it on
their heads. Then I saw the Green Man's face in Norwich
Cathedral, finely featured, intensely observing, haunting, and
recognized that the Church's triumphalism over the Old
Religion required some background reading. The poet William

Anderson reminds me that the Green Man is no enemy of Christ, nor would the Lord who walked among the foliage of Palestine have felt threatened by him. He who would die on the Tree used the great metaphors of nature to explain his Gospel, and the saints would do likewise. Hildegard of Bingen, with her interest in plants and her philosophy of *viriditas* – greenness – should be the patron saint of the Greens, and St Francis, of course, with his exquisite *Canticle of the Sun*, made it obvious to medieval churchmen that one should pray and praise via the natural as well as the supernatural. Not that some of them were too easy about this. I see them putting down the joy rising within them as the spring arrives, and as the font-makers put down the Green Man.

Preparing the first Lent matins, I always forget to change the Te Deum for the Benedicite. Mrs Cardy reminds me. For decades she has written out the services, chosen the settings, had a talk with me on the telephone every Thursday evening about the hymns and psalms and the fields which her husband ploughed and, at this moment, their greening. She has lived all her long life here and the leaves of her prayer-book and hymn-book, woodland and meadow, garden and graveyard have become interwoven. 'O all ye Green Things upon the Earth,' we sing, 'bless ye the Lord.' The transition of the Benedicite for the Te Deum was required by the Tudor prayer-book. The Reformers must have felt the first warm sun on their backs, seen the last of the winter. Enchanted by Brother Sun, Francis sat in the garden of San Damiano and wrote his green praise.

Consolation

Counterpoint. From the bedside radio, earthquake, crime, war, suffering people, suffering creatures. Downstairs, the tick of the clock, Max lapping, the wind playing a trombone in the chimney, a creeper rattling to come in, the sound of stream-water finding its way round the pipes. Given our current technology, it would all have been the same in 1595, fearful noises from afar, the life-beat of a particular house, they would have been set against each other. Huge pearly whorled shells among the flowerpots suggest that I am able to check if the sea still pounds the Indian shore – or was it Africa? They did tell me when I was ten. I hold one to my ear and listen to those hypnotic waves. I am consoled by the continuum of these and by less mysterious sonics.

The post arrives, plus the paper and the groceries and the stamps. It is well known that I am an outpost and must be provisioned. 'We don't forget you!' I should hope not. As it is well known too that a writer can do what he likes, I take my bow-saw to where the 1987 gale-wood still swings among the oaks – 'widow-makers' is what they call such branches in the Australian forests – and by use of a rope and admirable determination, I have enough logs until Easter. It is whilst tidying up these great trees that this comfortable word 'con-solation' creeps back into my head and I found myself hunting it through the years to when it made its first impact. It was when, long ago, I helped to rehouse a seventeenth-century library, once the property of Samuel Harsnett, Archbishop of York, and there, wrapped in an old copy of *The Times*, was Caxton's edition of a book which meant a lot to many genera-tions of Christians, putting their different predicaments into perspective and making rational and real the ultimate caring of

God. It was Boethius's *The Consolation of Philosophy*, like *Pilgrim's Progress*, the Letter to the Ephesians and *Mort D'Arthur*, a part of the literature which has come to us from the prison cell. Not only Caxton, but King Alfred translated the *Consolation* and the word itself, with its soft roll of vowels, provided a kind of linguistic assurance.

But not so much now. Barnabas, once the son of consolation, has become the son of exhortation, and in Romans the God of patience and consolation is now 'the source of all fortitude and encouragement'. But I'm glad to see that poor Job is still being harangued with, 'Does not the consolation of God suffice you?' I give notice that when my time comes I will not take kindly to being exhorted instead of consoled. How meticulously unconsoling is the News, how hard to feel what one should feel as it reels past.

Lent One: Our Airfield

'What I would like,' said the Australian guest, responding to my various offerings, 'is to hear a skylark.' Step right outside, I was about to answer, when I remembered our abandoned airfield. Although abandoned isn't quite the right adjective, since farmers and gliders have reclaimed it. However, if one wishes to hear skylarks at their zenith and creating what Marvell called 'the mosaic of the Air', then find a deserted World War Two airfield, or indeed any old battlefield, for they share the same exhilarating yet tragic ambience as well as a level earth and high heaven conjunction which larks themselves find particularly suitable for nests and songs. This week they were up over our ex-USAF 362 Fighter Group Airfield, ecstatic specks making a glorious noise above the wet corn and oilseed rape, the latter about to burst into flat Van Gogh yellow. I entered the airfield near the glider base to listen to them. Fragile machines lay in snowy rows by the new clubhouse. On Sundays they are persuaded from their trailer-chrysalises to soar in pure silence over our church service.

The great runways were torn up years ago and have long joined the commonwealth of rubble. But the perimeter roads remain, curving into views which do not seem to belong to our, or to any neighbouring, parish. Coltsfoot and artefacts from the big band era are squeezed into their cracks. The Americans arrived in Wormingford on St Andrew's Day 1943, which happened to be the village's patronal day, although it is generally accepted that the Pentagon hadn't planned this. I gazed once more at the memorial by the hedge on which the names of the dead are engraved in close lists, like items in an old account-book. There are a few captains but mostly they are lieutenants – the Monument of the One Hundred Lieutenants. Some have names – Troy Dean – which flick against the consciousness like those among the credits of a B-movie, briefly reinstating a young smile.

I walked west all the afternoon, passing Mr Hodge's fine lambs. It has been a bad, sodden, deathly spring for lambs but these have come through. Impeccable fields and set-aside fields, military neatness and rusty tackle, sticky-buds and, of course, larks. The skies are one vast unending parade of cloud. At the saluting-base I face a rotting stack and a felled oak. There are grooves for the flag-poles. Miles away the orange wind-sock of the Essex and Suffolk Gliding Club billows happily.

House Communion

And the first of our Lenten house-communions. Paul, who inaugurated them a decade or so ago, presides at a snowy table. We are in a fine new house on a bank and it stares directly across the river at the fine ancient house where Martin Shaw worked at his hymns. Between us all is wind and squall, blackness and solitude. It is a night to reflect on what happens when the sacraments are fetched from the altar to the tea-table. I think of all those – women especially – who through Christian history have aspired to re-create a Bethany or an Emmaus within their own homes. Given the choice, I would much have preferred being a guest in one of these than in those *sancta casi* flying about in Italy and Norfolk during the Middle Ages. At least I would know where I was.

The house-communion forces us to put our thinking-caps on, as teacher used to say. It possesses a different quiet to that in the chancel, and this is not due to soft furnishings. It has the quietness of a quiet room. Although everything is set out as the rubric requires, a table has been laid. Prayer rises from, and then fills, a home. For an hour or two nothing is secular, and certainly not the cat.

Houghton House, Ampthill, Bunyan's 'House Beautiful', which still skeletally stands facing his Delectable Mountains (the Chilterns), was in reality tragic, although he the literary genius mending its saucepans never knew it. But its inhabitants were to flee from it and leave it to rot. I remember climbing up to it and finding what he found, and had I not read its sad history I would have found nothing more. It was beautiful, even in ruin. Quite where Magdalen Herbert's house stood near Charing Cross nobody now knows, but by all accounts it must have been the ultimate Christian salon. All the best gardeners, all the best poets, all the best talk – and a splendid cuisine. Nobody said 'Let us pray', because its very hospitality was prayer. They all said the food was very good.

So it was in the little Suffolk houses of my boyhood which were too modest to know how holy they were. Yet their sacredness hangs around in my head like the click of needles, the big sigh which the old clock gave before it could summon up the strength to chime, and other interior sounds. My mentor where those simple country interiors are concerned is the writer Alison Uttley, a miniaturist who deals in great matters. We all consecrate our rooms without knowing it. On my deeds I read 'dwelling-house'. To dwell means to abide for a time. So make the most of it. The old home – its blessedness, its cantankerousness.

Lent Two

Like Robert Frost, I can say that 'I have been one acquainted with the night.' I may have to have special spectacles for television but outside my night-sight is such that I have never carried a torch. The gradations of darkness have become as noticeable to me as variations in the daylight. I would do more night walking, except that I don't like to panic roosting pheasants into flight like old protesting Blenheim bombers, or to do anything which could trouble the dear horses grouped in tender equilibrium under the sloe hedge. But I enjoy a ringing step on a night road and making out the broken-backed roofs of ancient farms, and searching ploughed hills which at such a

moment could be going up and up until they become alps. At night local towns identify their existence by drawing saffron streaks across the indigo. A rectangular blaze here and there in the blackness tells where the midnight oil is being spilt. The poet may not have seen what flowers were at his feet, but I can just make out my sumptuous Lenten roses (*Helleborus orientalis*). Badgers, foxes, rabbits and owls cough, hoot, bark and rustle.

A Quaker friend apprenticed to horse-farming in the thirties remembers his master getting up at two o'clock sharp every morning to reassure his beasts. A word here, a pat there. And I can recall the stockmen's lanterns as they made their rounds. 'Fareyouwell, then.' Max the cat will accompany me on these late strolls when he feels like it, now and then shinning up a tree to show off. On a light dark night I can just make out a Norman church whose windows, wrote Adrian Bell, 'are no more than dream holes, the wall so thick that the light has the effect of being poured in through a funnel'. Well, that is how they liked it, our ancestors, a bright Saviour in a richly gloomy cave.

I think of Moses' forty nights on that spent volcano Horeb,

and of his beseeching prayer, 'Show me thy glory.' Then I think of the Lord's forty nights in the cold hills from which he could see, perhaps, twinkling rushlights as the valley families went to warm beds. God's answer to Moses was 'I will make all my goodness pass before thee.' Evil's answer to Jesus was to show him from a mountain top an imperial way out of his dilemma. The Lord's resistance to what Cranmer so chillingly described as 'thoughts which may assault the soul' remains deeply lonely. As Moses and Jesus knew, it can be terrible to be wide awake in the dark.

Telling Each Other What We Know

It has long been the custom to feed me with information. Not too much all at once, of course. One mustn't tell everything one knows in a single outpouring. The Scheherazade method is preferable. A tale today and another next time we meet. Mr Chaplin, kindly driving me from matins to matins, tells me about the mount of Mount Bures and how, seventy years ago, it was covered in bluebells. 'People came to see it.' Was the moat filled with water then? 'Almost.' I am careful not to add my own facts. He would not appreciate having his bluebells trumped by archaeology. Perfectly dressed in a dark suit, he has been jangling a pair of bells which the village has listened to since Agincourt. He rolls slightly as he walks, like an old sailor, although he started work at the water-mill. He smokes his pipe to the penultimate limit when he comes to church, knocking it out against a fine tomb. There has been tragedy in his quiet life but as we both know all about this there is no occasion to mention it. We dart along through the Lenten lanes in his bright red car and the pheasants run and scatter. It is cold and leaden, the sky turning the winter wheat an acid green – the coldest winter, they say, for five years. The farmers are praying for ten mild, dry days of spring drilling, warmish but not soggy, friable – 'you know, Lord.' Mr Cowlin is my seedsman, that is, he doles out a few wonderful facts of his trade whenever we meet. Did I know, for instance, that those punnets of cress in the supermarkets isn't cress at all, but rape? 'Rape!' True. I think of the egg-and-cress sandwiches made from my own flannel-grown cress when I was a boy, and deplore the way the world is going. Where will it all end?

As you would imagine, Mount Bures stands on a prominence and I have to climb up out of the valley to reach it. As the castle mount is another forty feet, the views spread for miles. Less than two hundred souls live there. Its hours are measured by a nippy little train which frequently holds up the faithful when the crossing-gates are closed. This crossing used to be one of those classic railwaymen's gardens, with 'Mount Bures' spelled out in aubrietia long ago, and runner-beans climbing the danger sign, but now it is forlorn. Just a spot to rattle over.

My Lenten addresses are of the teaching sort. We have done the Creed and the Lord's Prayer, and soon we shall do the Psalms. When I look at the dear faces who have been saying these things for years and years, I think, what an impertinence! For me to explain them, that is. But they settle back like children in class. My object is to put a brake on the liturgy – to give its recitation a check and a meaning. As Herbert said, 'Hurry is the death of prayer.'

Lent Three

Follow God 'as dear children', says the Lenten epistle, 'walk as children of light.' Some thirty children of light, or of Great Tey Primary School, as they are generally recognized, have walked down the track for an art lesson, have left their muddy shoes on the doorstep like Muslims, and have sat on the farmhouse floor in their socks. Sparks from the split willow burning on the hearth fly all around them and there is a happy sense of terror. These children are part of our 'cluster' or amalgamation of Church of England Aided schools in the area, and they brought four well-behaved teachers with them. These too have removed their shoes and I feel I should take mine off in common homage to scrubbed bricks. What with so many trails of little feet and clouds of glory, I find myself temporarily nonplussed. All these fair upturned faces, all these imploring hands which have to be gently ordered down. 'Does everybody here like painting and drawing?' A universal yes. Isn't it easily the best thing one can do? Wild agreement. The lesson starts. I tell them the story of John Nash who lived in this old house, and how he sketched in the fields come rain, come shine. Or, if it was impossible to get out, how he would sit in a window painting snow, which is harder than you might think.

We move back to two other artist-boys from the neighbourhood, Tom Gainsborough and John Constable, who fished in our river and played in its meadows, and look what happened to them! Who would like to be an artist? Everybody. Two days later the postman brings a much-signed letter of thanks, plus a fine picture of my house. It is the house we all draw at the beginning, with windows hanging from the eaves like flags and hospitable chimneys. As for myself, I am now part of a Project and must be revisited, although next time on a sunny day with a packed lunch. They will tell me when.

More clouds of glory when I go to our own village school, c. 1870, and scarcely a flint missing. They wreath around the computer screens and up to where the oil-lamps used to swing. This is a state visit in my role as governor. As ever, time-caught and inescapable, I can hear vanished generations droning out their tables, dates and prayers, the Lord's Prayer itself a master-piece of incomprehension. Soon, as I knew I must, I am accompanied to the rain gauge and to mystical meteorological signs on the asphalt. 'The clouds are cumulus,' says the nine-year-old. 'So they are!' I say, truly enlightened.

St Chad

The north wind has come to chill us to the bone. It is official. It grins witheringly at the central heating and pierces its way into ancient and new dwellings. But not through the bright plastic armour of the ramblers, presumably, or they would never have dared to tread on the high ground. There they go, loners or groupies, crackling along, watching for fieldfares, halting to listen to the woodpecker chopping away at my oak. They call out in brave voices. The early cyclists, too, spin along the B-roads in their hideous lycra gear, picking up the sweet music of tyre on tarmac through the drowning gale.

In church I announce the week of prayer for Christian unity. 'How these weeks for this or that come round,' they say. Unity to us has some of the beautiful impossibility of the leopard lying down with the kid. But of course we must pray that it might be possible. For those of us who keep an eye on what might be called unity at large, our wishfulness has not been helped by the news that the Pope and the Patriarch are still unable to visit each other. Scarcely less hazy to us 800 inhabitants of three old villages is the administrative fact of our being a united benefice when it is as plain as the nose on your face that we are Wormingford, Mount Bures and Little Horkesley. What is united about this? All the same, we know our Christian duty and are capable of selfless gestures towards each other, such as attending each other's special celebrations, flower shows and the like, whilst never abandoning our own distinctiveness. This last being another impossibility, as we have never been able to discover quite what it is. All that we are certain of is that a millennium of parish entity has created a look, a feeling, an attitude, a geography, and thus an act of worship, if you like, which is indigenous, and can be either the strength or the despair of the recent groupings. When a parishioner says, 'We love our church,' he is being honest. He loves a sight and a sound which may have been with him since childhood, or which spoke to him acceptingly later on. He is not a fool and he understands that it is but a fraction of a greater sight and sound, but it is the fraction which is *his*. Christian unity to him is an abstract ideal. A united benefice to him has more to do with diocesan bookkeeping than the collective spirit. Always, always, 'his heart is in the right place,' either Wormingford . . . etc. Never in three places at once.

All the same, we are a unification of historic groups. Drawn into the congregations of all three churches are Scots Presbyterians, Baptists, Methodists and people whose prayer life we know nothing about, some local, some from towns. They rarely say why or how.

Cathedral Camps

To Southwark in the biting cold. Trees rattle and snap on the way and little rivers freeze in their valleys. Eventually, the splendours of Liverpool Street which is full of chattering school parties so that it sounds like an aviary. The teachers have warm velvety hats jammed down over their ears. The children are apparently winter-proof and are seated on the concourse like waiting armies. Soon they will storm the V. & A. The Thames is high and sullen at London Bridge, swirling grumpily along. Homeless youths huddle out of the wind.

I am early for the meeting in the Chapter House so I call on old friends. First Lancelot Andrewes, who could claim to be the father of the school outing because he liked to walk and teach at the same time. Crocodiles of Westminster boys would be led along the river by their charismatic headmaster, and droning their Latin and Greek. But here he lies in Southwark Cathedral, gaudy yet wonderfully serious, and clearly very tired. Next, Edmund Shakespeare, William's baby brother, aged 27 when they laid him here. Did he come up from Warwickshire to try his luck in town? What carried him off? William would have come to his funeral and dropped the handful of grave-dirt on to the coffin. A little later he would write *Cymbeline* in which one brother mourns another:

> Fear no more the heat o' the sun,
> Nor the furious winter's rages;
> Thou thy worldly task hast done,
> Home art gone and ta'en thy wages.
> Golden lads and girls all must,
> Like chimney-sweepers, come to dust.

73

It is our biannual Cathedral Camps meeting when we discuss the organization of the summer cleaning of many cathedrals by young people. It is a great business. Off they go in parties of fifteen to twenty to dust, polish, record and mend, and also to enjoy themselves. Monuments, carvings, architecture, glass, often the kind of things which until recently are rarely cleaned, are left spotless. O all ye deans and provosts, bless ye the Lord, and say thank you, too, to your delightful visitors. Between meetings we attend a Lenten Eucharist. The high altar is hung with sackcloth and the epistle is from the contrite *Song of the Three Holy Children*. We are sad and thoughtful, and also pleased to be old friends who find each other here every few months, and all part of a calendar which interlocks with the Calendar. 'Who sweeps a room, as for thy laws . . .'

The Annunciation

A wild March afternoon at Little Henny, our neighbour village. It has its head in clouds and its feet in streams. Every kind of weather is chasing through it. We can see it coming in, the hail, the stiff rain, the surprising bursts of sunny warmth, the bouts of iciness. Having just sung the incomparable 'My song is love unknown' at the Lenten service (a *frisson* of delight when it was announced), Alan and I have gone in search of its author Samuel Crossman, rector here ages ago. We tramp through the March mud of what was not a happy living. The locals soon got rid of him. His church is now no more than a mark in a field. The deep lanes through which he would have

walked only just take the car. Huge creamy bosses of primroses light the ditches, and magpies rush ahead of us. There is a scattering of houses, nothing more. If it is excitement you are after you must go to Great Henny. When I was a boy the Sudbury Boat Club would row down the Stour to Great Henny on Good Friday morning for beer and hot cross buns. But we,

Alan and I, are at this moment elevated above such earthy sprees. We are where a dejected young seventeenth-century clergyman evidently sought solace in Herbert's *The Temple*, his querulous congregation having turned him out of theirs. Herbert's poems include one entitled 'Love Unknown' and his majestic meditation 'The Sacrifice' contains the line 'Never was grief like mine' which Crossman uses in his hymn.

Except it wasn't a hymn at the beginning. It was one of a handful of verses called *The Young Man's Meditation*, and as this little book was published soon after its author left Little Henny, one may presume that it took shape in its lanes and vanished church. It being such buffeting and exhilarating weather, with the puddles shining and the birds singing against a gale, I granted us licence to listen to Parson Crossman's words about the cruelty of the world and the love which overrides it. 'My Song' is a strong and uncomfortable statement about humanity's ability to turn on what is good, what is right. Priest–poets such as Crossman, fine minds in uncouth livings, would have been alarmed by the illumination they continue to shed.

Crossman departed from Little Henny in 1662 and had to bide his time. Shortly after the First World War, when the *English Hymnal* was being edited, Geoffrey Shaw took the composer John Ireland out to lunch. Half-way through it he handed a slip of paper across the table with 'I need a tune for this lovely poem.' Ireland read it and reread it, then wrote for a few minutes on the back of the menu. 'Here is your tune.' The words and the music now possess Henny's hilltop, homing there after three centuries.

Mothering Sunday

Mothering Sunday, and the days leading to it have been blissful, bringing everything out, as they say. On a sudden impulse I clambered to the summit of the 'mount' of Mount Bures to get a Norman sentinel's view of things. Ten miles of springtime. Tributary streams, still very full because of all the rain, and the give-away humps and lines of a long-lost garden. Also a grey goose and a grey goat attended by a youth, all quite still. Hidden from him but plain to me are the graves of his brother and sister, who died in road accidents. Below, the moat is not much more than a damp saucer sprinkled with celandine. Which lord ordered this earth-castle to be piled up, Sackville . . . de Vere? No one knows. Blackberries and bluebells have conquered it. The futility of so much of what we are made to do. Why do half the things we do, questioned Traherne, when one could sit under a tree?

But Maisie Pettican has been her ever-reliable hard-working self, and has made a great many small nosegays for the Mothering Sunday service. I pile them on the altar and the delicate April scent permeates the interior. During the last hymn – Stewart Cross's 'Father, Lord of all Creation' – boys and girls carry the yellow, green and white bunches to the singing women. 'But what if she isn't a mother?' – *sotto voce* once. 'Never you mind.' This year I reduce the folklore, which I reckon they must by now know by heart. Instead, I steer in the direction of today's Epistle and Gospel, which are full of intriguing undercurrents, the first being about 'children of promise' and the second about the boy who had his packed lunch miraculously turned into a huge picnic. His mother, I felt it safe to surmise, would have baked those five loaves. There are people present whose mothers would have been baking for them seventy years ago or more. I discover in an antediluvian guide which came with my mother's first gas-stove, a recipe for a simnel-cake but wisely do not give it out from the pulpit.

Francis Kilvert is the poet of church flowers. Some years ago I walked from Bronydd to Clyro to sit on the tombstone where on a March afternoon in 1871 he watched a spider 'scuttling over the sacred words and memories' and listened, unseen, to 'subdued village voices'. His flower-finder was Miss Sandell, 'who taught me more about them in ten minutes than I have learnt from books in all my life'.

Lent Five

'Of this parish', I say, reading the banns. The future bride who, although resident here for years has made a courteous first visit to the church in order to hear them, starts at this mention of her parochiality. She had not seen herself so localized. And then there are those who regularly worship in all three parishes but are not 'of' any one of them. Some of them drive through quite a lot of parishes *en route*, closing their ears to seductive bells and their eyes to little waves which say 'join us'. No fear; we are driving to where we feel we belong, we extra-parochials. Our cars have broken every barrier down. Well, welcome, welcome. Car-less, I have to take what is offered, like those who lived in this house for centuries. But it does more or less straddle the boundaries so that I can jump across a ditch from one village to the next, or if it comes to that I can walk down the field and cross the river from Essex into my native Suffolk. So an extravagant choice.

Beneficially, we are united on paper and in our hearts, but not parochially. Who can be? It is asking too much. All the same we are very Christian and think nothing of occasional excursions across a boundary to help out with our neighbour's festival or anthem. And also, let it be said, with funds. At the same time we know our place – especially those who have driven ten or more miles to it – and an inexpressible happiness fills us as our own tree-held tower looms at the end of the lane. Our congregations are affectionate yet distinctive, our ringers are regular yet flighty, being easily led creatures who think nothing of crossing England to attempt a peal. But they nail up their honours in the home church.

My grandparents could remember 'the flight from the land' when huge numbers of indigenous people 'got off the land', as they themselves put it. Rider Haggard, in his moving inventory of an agricultural disaster, prefaced his book with a quotation from Judges – 'The highways were unoccupied . . . the inhabitants of the villages ceased.' Now we have those who are 'of this parish' without knowing it. They say that they live in the country and work in town. One might glimpse them mowing on a Sunday, although habitually they are far slyer than Rupert Brooke's rural dean.

Thomas Ken, Bishop of Bath and Wells

It is the day of Mr Paddon's two-yearly visitation and those of us who are not on the mains have been pulling up our watery socks. He comes to sample our bacteria, to marvel that we are still alive and have not been washed into oblivion by our medieval supply. The Bottengoms water has never frozen in the coldest winters or dried up in the hottest summers. What is also remarkable is its ability to spring from the ground and then from my taps – and then towards the river – all within a couple of hundred yards of its origin to its final disappearance in the valley. Thankfully, Mr Paddon is pleased with me for having carried out his last recommendations to the letter and we are able to resume our various water memories before he sets off on his bacterial mission to The Grange and to The Hall, both a mile from the mains and, like me, drinking from the same source which refreshed centuries of their inhabitants. As with these ancients, I have to share a stream with foxes, badgers and, I suspect, Max the cat, but it flows fast and constantly, so let us hope that it bears all their impurities away. My chief anxiety is that it shouldn't worry Mr Paddon once every two years. His exciting news is that he has found a Victorian well in his garden and, after he had cleared it of twenty feet of rubble, found four feet of pure water too. Does he drink it? He eyed me warily. He is on the mains.

The Gospels being so full of wells it was no wonder that hydrolatry became popular. Worshipping water seemed an obvious thing to do. Water was never simply water, it was different wherever one found it, especially holy if a saint lived near by, particularly medicinal if it coursed through certain rocks. The writer James Rattue adds another reminder: 'In pools of water the human being first saw his own face, and could see the world mirrored around him: and this is perhaps the most surprising and extraordinary power of water.' As I read this I thought of Thomas Traherne's magical poem *Shadows in the Water* in which a boy staring into a puddle 'chanc'd another World to meet'.

> . . . what can it mean?
> But that below the purling Stream
>   some unknown Joys there be
>   Laid up in Store for me;
> To which I shall, when that thin Skin
> Is broken, be admitted in.

Wells which contained mineral properties which soothed sore eyes were called 'sunrising-water'. It is Passiontide, the days of suffering which precede the Redemptive Death, when Christ went down into the depths.

Passion Sunday

I precede the intercessions with a 'First a time of silence' and could hear a pin drop. In one old church we all listen to twigs tapping at the window, though not for more than a minute. We are not Quakers and are disconcerted by corporate soundlessness. Should it continue it will run into November 11th, and then where will we be! We are so suggestible. Paul's dramatic conversion suggests to me my first encounter with the wonderful name 'Damascus', which wasn't in Acts but in my father's reminiscence of walking along that selfsame road

– behind General Allenby. All so long ago. My favourite part of the Paul story is that insistent 'why are you travelling in this direction?' and his blinding understanding that the official answer would not do. At some moment or other conscience makes heretics of us all, to the great inconvenience of religion.

But that silent church when the music stops and the people have gone, and the clock rumbles into a chime, what a questioning church it is. R. S. Thomas's sublime account of what is occurring when nothing is going on, as we say, I always think should hang in every vestry. Silence speaks to the priest – to that left-alone figure turning off heat and light, indeed – and whoever is last one out there can be that question, 'Why are you doing this?' 'Is this where God hides/From my searching?' asks the poet–priest.

> I have stopped to listen,
> After the few people have gone,
> To the air recomposing itself
> For vigil.

It is neither a prickly nor a resounding silence which goads my imagination when, as I often do, I take a seat in the empty church. But it has its complications, it being active, not negative. The silence says, 'It is a nuisance your knowing so much history; it distracts you from what I am telling you.' All over the world the temples are saying, 'Listen to this, it is my silence. Have you heard anything like it?'

Palm Sunday

Temperature-wise, hardly a time for movement, more a time to hug the hearth. But movement there undoubtedly is, at last a 'something doing' on the land. Modern farming has brought about such a desertion of the fields and meadows that the sight of John on the harrow and Peter's men at work on a vast onion-bed halts one in one's tracks. 'Look! People!' No good waving. We are in the car and no one is recognizable in a car. But we do slow down to rejoice in the old hullabaloo of tumbling earth, a thousand screaming gulls and a single human being involved in the great rite of sowing. And all this on the floor of the valley, once a deer-park and every other year a flood, but now sown, and no wonder, for the rich alluvial soil looks as though it could grow harvests overnight.

After a costly stop at the market garden – new secateurs etc. – Alan and I jog along through the deep Little Cornard lanes meeting every kind of spring-farming vehicle and agricultural implement, so there is much backing to allow them to scrape past. The friable-soil days have come at last. The lovely lane past Peacock Hall, the gaunt apple orchards which in no time will be in blossom, and where there is water, palm willow or the great sallow which until the import of the dry crosses now handed out on Palm Sunday, was what the Englishman cut down and metaphorically cast before his Lord. We always believed as children, and our grandparents all their lives, that 'sally' or 'pussy-willow' was what the ass trod as it bore its sacred rider up the steep hill to the Temple. Branches of it stood in pots in the classroom until the gold-dust fell from the silky catkins and leaves began to sprout. It was gathered from the river banks and given out in the church porch – Christ the King's catkins. The Palm Sunday procession was made from church to church, singing, of course, St Theodulf's magnificent hymn, *Gloria, laus et honor*, over and over again. He was one of Charlemagne's poet–bishops and, they say, the inventor of parish education and a keen advocate of beautifully illustrated Gospels. His hymn shows him a master of exultation. By rights we should surge up to the church, then into it, singing it, and all very grandly – 'To thee now high exalted, our melody we raise.' Just one week after his triumphal entrance, the risen Lord walked in a garden, a simple quiet place where the tombs were made. The spiritual as well as the natural movement of these March–April days is immense and irresistible. We are swept along, though far from mindlessly. There is planting, there is purpose, there is intelligence.

Selling Up

'Farm for Sale' – two of them actually, but no property-agents' boards in the fields. Huge chunks of the village will discreetly change hands but so far as the landscape is concerned little will alter. The new buyers are not likely to spread orchards where the wheat flourished, although once they did, and not so long since either. I sometimes think that farmers would need to plant bananas to make today's villager stop the car and take in the local agricultural view. Escaped rape is growing outside the hedge and a neighbour pointed out the 'broccoli', whilst the postman earlier in the year saw my butterbur tufts and hazarded, 'lettuces?'

Many of our acres have been returned to grass and the

informed attitude of two of our farmers in particular to hedge-rows has gradually influenced the others, so the great sprawling workplace of Wormingford is at its best in May. It delights me, both for its personal associations and its loveliness. I want to tell everyone, the farmers too, 'Forget the Common Market *et al.* for an hour and look around you.' There is a limit to our springtimes, so take care never to miss one. The most celebrated farming wiseacre of all, Thomas Tusser, ploughed and sowed by our river – not very efficiently, I must confess, he being a musician by trade – yet his saws have become part of the language. Here is one which, understandably, has dropped out of usage: 'Some respite to husbands the weather may send, but housewives' affairs have never an end.' Eventually Tom Tusser sold up and went to Norfolk, exchanging the Stour for the Waveney. Whilst he struggled with his harvests two fellow musicians, William Byrd and Thomas Tallis, were collaborating on the motets which fill our cathedrals to this day.

Selling up a farm used to be a tragic business. It was called 'the coming down time' in East Anglia. Unlike the almost furtive exchange of ownership today, a farm sale was a quite unbearably public affair. The ruined man stood metaphorically naked before the parish, all his chattels and machinery, his beloved working horses and stock paraded in the yard, whilst his creditors totted up the lots. My old friend Hugh Barrett wrote the best account of such a sale I have ever read in his *Early to Rise: A Suffolk Morning.* He was a teenager when he witnessed it. Such ruined farmers often drowned or shot themselves. It all remains in living memory. Now the village hears whispers of millions. The middle-aged taxi-driver who began as a farm boy at Framlingham shakes his head.

Holy Week

Holy Week. The school has created a work of art for the church which leaves me staring. It is a corporate picture of painted eggs, but as these lack the ovate bulge the effect is one of Easter landscapes where whites and yolks are usually found. Strange, beautiful colours by various hands. What am I seeing? What hope the Tate Gallery, what hope the General Synod? This masterpiece is propped opposite a pillar on which a Tudor hand has scratched with antlers from the deer-park. I – name indecipherable – was here.

The sad days pass. I am static, seated down with work. But various Holy Week wanderings drift through my consciousness. I think of Etheria, the Freya Stark of her day, who in *c.* AD 380 set off from Spain for Jerusalem to write the proto-pilgrimage travel book, at least by a woman. There she found an elaborate liturgy in full swing and all intensely localized. And I think too of John Donne's guilty ride to Wales on Good Friday – he was on a visit to George Herbert's brother Edward – guilty because all day he faced west, geographically at least turning his back on 'that spectacle of too much weight for me'. Too much weight for any of us. Both Donne and Herbert, all the old writers, Julian included, appear to have their Crucifixion contemplation informed by the common sight of scaffolds. Not even our daily glut of filmed horrors from all over the world has quite the same effect as part-seeing, part-avoiding what is taking place on the gibbet just up the road. Donne's ride to Wales on Good Friday took place two years before his ordination and his poem is his apology to Christ for still facing both ways. In *The Agonie* George Herbert, with his hard descriptions of 'A man so wrung with pains, that all his hair,/his skin, his garments bloody be' and 'a pike' reminds his contemporaries that what they saw so commonplace at executions was what was seen at Calvary.

But Easter dawns. Herbert's lute – he was an excellent musician and folk would sometimes stop and listen as he sang to his own accompaniment in an otherwise empty church – has become an instrument daringly devised from wood taken from the Cross and its strings made of those poor stretched sinews. In the seventeenth century sacred music was always played at a higher pitch than secular music.

> His stretched sinews taught all strings, what key
> Is best to celebrate this most high day.

Easter Eve

L ike many people tied to an official calendar I tend to operate an unofficial one in tandem with it. Orthodoxy has a way of starting hares. There cannot be many more Easters before the locals discover that I am much attached to the Emmaus story, which is the Gospel for Easter Monday. But who would hear it then? A voice from a faraway teacher is heard saying 'freely translate', and so the congregation has to listen to it, year after year, on Easter Eve. This is, after all, the evening of the day of the Lord's Resurrection when he caught up with his frightened followers, and in whose house the first evensong was sung. But only after he had been recognized in the breaking of bread. The stranger guest had become the familiar host. There used to be little country chapels all over Suffolk when I was a boy on whose shiny black notice-boards was painted in gold, 'Lord's Day, Breaking of Bread. 11 a.m.'

I have been invited to visit Credenhill, Thomas Traherne's parish. I can scarcely believe it. Just as I have a personal calendar, so I have a private map, and Credenhill is well marked as an Emmaus. Traherne, the youthful rector, instructing his pupil Mrs Hopton in the basics of Christianity, was unnerved by the Herefordshire night:

Another time, in a lowering and sad evening, being alone in the field, when all things were dead and quiet, a certain want and horror fell upon me, beyond imagination. The unprofitableness and silence of the place dissatisfied me, its wideness terrified me, from the utmost ends of the earth fears surrounded me. How did I know but dangers might suddenly arise from the east?

Traherne then became convinced that he had been 'made to hold a communion with the secrets of divine providence' and that he could be assured of 'the comfort of houses and friends'.

I used to walk in Cornwall at Easter, usually keeping to a radius of my friend the poet James Turner's house, but now and then getting so far from home that the hospitable axial became lost. Where was I? Where was 'home'? Once I was on the vast headland of Pentire with the Trevose lighthouse flashing through the fog. Once I was striding along to Egloshayle in a salty wind and hearing church bells far up the Camel. This road was said to be haunted by a white rabbit which dogged the benighted traveller's heels and could not be shaken off. A traveller who tried to shoot it – shot himself. Our Suffolk wilds are haunted by a hound named Shuck. My track is haunted by a big black cat who would do anything for a tin of Whiskas.

Easter Saturday

The constancy of the natural world (admitting a few breaks and aberrations) is a daily balance to the News. 'Bees gather' reported the Reverend Gilbert White, and almost to the hour some 230 years on so they do around the sallows here. They are but the van of a humming army which will invade this flowery hollow from the local hives. Elspeth's bees from Water Lane, bees from Honey Hall, Mount Bures, Harold's bees from Coronilla, Rosie's bees, Charles's bees, social bees and solitary bees.

An ancient man who had been
Young here arrived to say,
'Mother saw to the flowers, of course.'
Of course. Father saw to that.
Their ancient son spoke of hives.
Hives here? 'Hives, honeybees,
Pears in the orchard, muck
In the soil. All you had to have.'

Our first close sighting of them was on the treacle-tin. There they were, hiving in a poor dead lion, the lion which Samson killed with his bare hands and afterwards used as a honey-pot. 'Out of the strong came forth sweetness' as Tate and Lyle said. I now watch them on the pussy-willow which we used to cut for Palm Sunday. Honey, honeycomb, beeswax, how Christianity has lived off both the products and the lesson of the social bee. In Charsfield church, where I used to worship, they rang a medieval bell on which was inscribed, 'Box of sweet honey, I am Michael's bell'. At the Easter Vigil here we shall acknowledge the bees' role in the liturgy:

Therefore, in this favourable time, accept, Oh holy Father, the evening sacrifice of this lighted candle which at this time thy holy Church maketh before thee, and offereth to thee by hands of thy servants, the work of the bees, thy creatures . . . For the wax that melteth doth but feed the flame, there-unto have the creatures of God's hand brought it forth, that it should give light in darkness.

The bees were the first to know of a death in the family when we were children. Someone would walk to the bottom of the garden where the hives were, bend down and say, 'John is dead.' Should a bee get into a room, it was let out most respectfully. A memory: a cool beeswaxed room containing sweetpeas being opened first thing in the morning. A matchless scent. Soon our bees will be working the rape, the borage, the orchards, and setting the cucumbers.

Easter One

Low Sunday takes me straight to the high ground – via the road to Emmaus. The story entrances me. Mark tells it laconically; not much to entrance there. But Luke! What a haunting addition to the Resurrection narrative. His version has everything that journeying man can ask for, from the mystery of being on the road at all to the fact that in spite of so much evidence to the contrary, he is likely to receive some human hospitality as well as divine companionship at the end of it. No one except the man who made the maps for my childhood Bible seems to be sure where Emmaus was. I owe him gratitude for providing me with an acceptable means for not listening to the sermon. Hazlitt's ancient father spent his old age lost in the interminable journeys of Israel – 'glimmering notions of the patriarchal wanderings, with palm-trees hovering in the horizon, and the processions of camels at the distance of three thousand years . . . My father's life was comparatively a dream; but it was a dream of infinity and eternity, of death, the resurrection, and a judgement to come!' My pretty map sets Emmaus in the Delilah–Samson country, but of course Emmaus is the home village to which we all retreat when we are led to believe that there is nowhere else to go. Those depressed walkers – who were they? Not two of the Eleven – that is made certain. And from the start, how pedestrian our Faith. Also – and here I am taking a map out of the Reverend Mr Hazlitt's atlas – where would the third walker have found himself had he not accepted that exquisite invitation, 'Abide with us, for it is toward evening, and the day is far spent'? In Jaffa, says my infant Bible.

Walking to read Ante-Communion on Good Friday, I was battered breathless by the spring gale which had already brought down my telephone line and showers of horse-chestnut candles. The scarecrow which John had stuck in the field next to the church was shockingly animated and bloated with the wind. It amused the crows breakfasting at its feet. As an old friend used to say, and not about birds, 'Nobody is frightened of nothing any more.' The violence of the day was in wild harmony with the violence of the hour. The weather forecasters were solicitous and talked of seventy-miles-an-hour hurricanes which they hoped would not spoil the holiday.

Staying at Home

Fortunate the writer or artist whose parish is his universe. I dare say there were those who urged George Mackay Brown to get about a bit, to leave Orkney and see the world, but he famously never did. We were long-distance friends, the kind of writers who originally began to absorb each other's landscape by osmosis. He never saw mine, except on the page, but once I flew off to Kirkwall without saying that I was coming, and there was his exactly as he said it would be. I travelled from Kirkwall to Stromness on Mr Peace's bus, and there was George walking towards me along the granite street in a cutting wind. 'I was told someone had arrived,' he said. We had tea by a big coal fire using 'Mother's best cups' and with myself taking in as much as I could of his work-den of a house when he wasn't looking, the cliff of books, the curly lino, the single photograph, the kitchen table which was his desk and the rocking-chair which was where he 'interrogated silence', as he put it. 'What a mercy God had taught us how to write,' he observed. 'What else would we have been fit for?' We talked of Thomas Hardy and how, in the morning, I was to sail to Hoy. A few yards away the sea was churning in the harbour and I remember thinking, 'How amazing! I am in Hamnavoe!' This was the old name for Stromness which George used to give himself a kind of elbow-room in time.

He died a few days ago, and just in time to get himself buried on the feast of St Magnus in Kirkwall Cathedral, that rose-coloured shrine built all at once during the twelfth century in contrition for a murder. There are only three great works of architecture in Orkney, St Magnus' Cathedral and the Rings of Brogar and Stenness, the latter over 4,000 years old, yet in their sharp-edged brightness not ancient at all, but like airy temples just awaiting a congregation. What strange hymns were sung here? Not far away was Skara Brae, a group of fully furnished cottages *c.* 3000 BC. Stone cupboards, seats, tables – everything still as it would have been when the family set out for the service at Stenness. George himself moved from age to age, and from island to island at will, and as the fancy took him. His Orcadians were given a time-span plus a timelessness, so that they were never cut off from their past or denied their own kind of ruthless present. He was an astringent poet–story-teller. One could imagine him in a post-Viking monastery, not very useful except for prayer and words. St Magnus' Cathedral has its own little poets' corner – Edwin Muir, Eric Linklater, the Saga writers – and now George. He was profoundly Christian, a writer who knew his place. His bones lie in the high kirkyard where I sat after we said farewell.

Brutal Realities

The great quandary of those who write about the country-side, or who paint it, is how to keep the euphoric vision, if not out of the general picture entirely, in its proper place. Such a vision of rural life is always in demand – always has been. When that peerless village poet John Clare wrote his *Shepherd's Calendar* his publishers demanded far less reality and much more charm. These thoughts occurred to me as, by coincidence, I wrote a fresh Introduction to Mary Russell Mitford's classic *Our Village* as the beef crisis deepened. This delightful book has acquired something of the reputation of being, like John Constable's paintings, the euphoric vision exemplified. Stick to such blissful scenes and you will never encounter the nasty woodshed, let alone be tempted to look inside it. No worse injustice to the writer and the artist could be offered. Each of them knew more than enough about village life to pretend that it was paradisaical, but they also knew that the essential happiness of humanity should still be found there in some shape or form, and that their own glimpses of it should be revealed in their work. Constable painted against the agricultural ruin and distress which followed the Napoleonic wars, Mitford's horror during her flower-gathering walks was having to pass the workhouse.

April 1996 will always be remembered as the time when the modern management of 'all ye Beasts and Cattle' – for make no mistake, every creature which we eat, fish, fowl and cow, is ethically as well as medically involved – cracked. Whatever the politicians and farmers do, and it will take years of repair, things will never be quite the same again. Unlike Mitford, when I walk I do not have to skirt the poor folk rotting away in the workhouse, and unlike Constable, whose uncles and aunts lived in Wormingford, I do not have to watch desperate labourers firing ricks, but I do know enough about certain forms of today's farming that when I pass some spots I have to weigh the practice against the cost. Villages are intriguing because they combine the most free-ranging gossip with the utmost reticence. Some things are always talked about, some things never. They also contain many new inhabitants who wouldn't be able to tell wheat from barley, as the saying goes, and for whom nothing is going on so far as they can see, agriculturally speaking. Such incomers through no fault of their own will never be able to understand the farmer himself, and his unique suffering at this moment. Christianity's most tender imagery comes from sheep. Beatrix Potter, famous sheep farmer as well as immortal animal-image maker, observed that 'every lamb that is born, is born to have its throat cut'.

Our Shop

The retention of the village post-office-shop has of late become *the* rural essential. This vanished, and all is lost. Ours has been tottering on the brink of oblivion for some time and since it is the only store for several miles in all directions, we have been holding our breath, myself particularly as it has been a crucial part of the economy of Bottengoms Farm since the days when the order included paraffin oil. Now all is saved. Faithful Margaret has succeeded in passing on the business, and the familiar little place will continue to buzz with our wants. The news deserves a peal of bells. There are villages round here *sans* post-office-shop, *sans* school, *sans* pub, *sans* much going on in the church beyond a monthly Communion, *sans*, really, the right to style themselves 'village' any more. I preach, though not in the pulpit, the duty of us all to buy things in the village shop, to visit it weekly and to enjoy it for what it is when in good hands, a holiday from the supermarket.

The crisis brought to mind for the first time that the very first shop I entered was undoubtedly a classic village store, that of Mr Jacob. It was five minutes' pram journey along the lane and was not one of your ill-stocked little dens profiteering on fire-sticks and lemonade crystals, but an adequate grocer's and hardware supplier for those who couldn't get into the local market town. Silvery cake-tins, sides of bacon, boiled sweets in tall glass jars, cigarettes, ham on the bone, fish from Lowestoft on Fridays. And an urgent notice which said, 'You may telephone from here.' Returning to that Suffolk churchyard recently, I saw Mr and Mrs Jacob's matrimonial tomb and imagined their large, kind faces looming across the counter to see the new baby. A few years later we would visit their shop to buy celluloid windmills, gob-stoppers and to 'give the order'. At Bottengoms the order says simply 'tea', 'cheese', 'razor-blades' or whatever, and the right brand always arrives, as though by magic.

There are no shops in scripture, only markets, as one would expect in the East. The five thousand were a long way from a market, hence their plight. They must have been spellbound to have followed their new teacher to where there wasn't a bite to eat and until hunger caused them to yearn for warm bread and delicacies and market-stalls. Listening to Easter reminiscences of Jerusalem, tourist after tourist confessed how the stones of the city overwhelmed them by their sacred association, and how the stoniness of the countryside shocked them. Aridity. It is something which even a green English village has to guard against.

Easter Two

Nora for the day. She is ninety-smudge, no longer counting time. She has been coming to the house since the war, once striding down the track, but now pushed by me through the sopping garden. Young friends have driven her from London. Their eyes are full of love for her. She danced with Karsavina in 1919. Now she sits by the blazing hearth in an enormous black fur coat with black Max on her lap. I can see him marvelling at the infinite variety of bliss. Nora is autobiographical, but only in private snatches. This suits me. Just a sentence or two, that's enough. She holds out her palms to the fire and the rings glitter. 'I once saw Karsavina standing all alone in the middle of the road at – Maidenhead! I couldn't believe it. I ran to her. "Oh, Madame, Madame . . ." she took me in her arms. "My child, my child . . ."' I realized that I would always see these Russian ladies in their surprised embrace. I pick marsh marigolds from the pond, and headily scented osmanthus for her to take back to Finchley. She makes a long journey to the piano to remind it that she has not forgotten their old association. Farewell, old friend.

On Thursday, a trip to Norfolk in blinding rain for a Lifeboat Literary Luncheon. Drenched gorse burns orange on the heath, wild angelica shoots along the wayside. Geoffrey Grigson used to say that its umbels seem to have been dipped in claret. Blythburgh Church is a gaunt stone casket above the marshes. Inside, the painted angels will be clinging to the rafters like the butterflies I find wintering in my curtains. Lowestoft looks as though it is made of carbon. Then the holiday-camp and that universe of the retired who never stop working – and who never ask for pay. Governments splutter about the expense of pensioners but do they ever cost what they do for society once

97

they are free of the office or wherever? The Church too costs 'giving' but cannot assess what is really given week after faithful week by those who care for its goods and services, many quite poor but who never ask for a penny. As I gaze across a sea of faces to talk about the East Anglian coast, I am seeing the practical, generous folk, few of them youthful, who toil for the Royal National Lifeboat Institution. Squalls howl about the roof. It would not have amazed me if a boat had to arrive from the shore to rescue us. 'Buffeting' is suitably found in the Epistle – 'For what glory is it, when ye be buffeted for your faults, ye shall take it patiently?' All the rest for the second Sunday after Easter is a pastoral, of course.

St George

Having done the weekly shopping, I rest among the tombs. Low clouds have hidden the sun for days and it is chilly. Below me spreads a scene which strikes a reminiscent chord, but of what? A group of youths and girls are drinking wine in the ruins of a Norman priory, the first house, to be exact, of the English Augustinians, and built with Roman bricks. Supermarket bottles glint in the roofless chancel and a joyful dog bounds through the aisles. Then I remember. It is one of those Forum scenes beloved of eighteenth-century artists when they visited untidy, unexcavated Italy. The idling figures, the inconsequence, the past glory. The eternal. The happy dog becomes framed in a high window and everybody stands up to beg it to come down. 'He always was aggravating,' says a boy. 'More wine?' Beneath his feet sleep the priors.

Bernard, Barrie, Chris and the others have been giving ringing lessons to some Americans from Honolulu who, having been presented with the bells of a Shrewsbury church, are here to learn what to do with them. 'They reckon there'll not be another peal for 2,000 miles,' says Barrie. Here it is thought odd if there are not bells every three miles.

Between services we picnic at Arger Fen. It is the annual bluebell party when we drink wine under tall freshly leaved trees and listen to the nightingales. These have never deserted Arger Fen, as they have my woodland. So here we are, friends from childhood and their children, Cambridge botanists, lads from the pub, gallant old women who brave the spring winds and the kind of damps which bluebells love, and strangers who stroll from one group to the next explaining who they are. This bluebell gathering is a hallowed rite, come rain or shine. To cry off because of the weather is thought feeble. The flowers themselves bloom in their millions and create an undulating cerulean forest carpet, its blue light 'beating up', as Gerard Manley Hopkins, poet of the bluebell, put it. It was he who was able to describe its curious sound as well as its breathtaking scent. 'The stalks rub and click . . . making a brittle rub and jostle like the noise of a hurdle strained by leaning against it.' The bluebell is the wild hyacinth known as '*non-scriptus*' because its petals are not marked with that sound of grief, AI, AI, as is the flower which grew from the blood of Hyacinthus.

Easter Three: St Mark

All is changed, all is new. The spring has come. The goal-posts are being taken down and the creases marked on the young grass. We are in the pavilion for the AGM, not of the sports committee but the PCC. It could lay claim to being one of the most delightful rooms in the village, with its group photographs of snowy players, larky pictures of the annual raft race on the river and its air of determined timelessness. Members of the cricket team creep in and out like mice as we make and unmake school governors and deanery representatives. And indeed ourselves. Another picture dominates this capable scene. It is of Brian Lara kissing the pitch in Antigua, although the general feeling is that the pitch should have risen up and kissed him. Brilliant April hedges can be seen through the window, so too can a devout figure painting white lines. Blessed is the management of pavilion and vestry. The chairman spins us through the agenda – 'I should be used to it be now, I've done it enough times' – and we propose and second with wild authority. The great art is to see that those who can do things don't resign. But the treasurer pleads for deliverance after so many years. What a loss. He stares at us from the platform and from various frames in which he clings to his bat. He tries to get off the PCC itself but we soon put a stop to that. Terrible things are happening. Elder is sprouting from the church gutter, the trapdoor used by the weekly clock-winder is actually a death-trap. There are songs from homing birds. Interregnums are good for you, Alan Webster used to say, and he was right. Looking around at us, a small, able group, such as quietly governs many a rural parish, there is no sign yet of things falling apart.

It will soon be Shakespeare's birthday – and death-day. To die on one's birthday, how strange. It is as though he was literally obeying his contemporary Joseph Hall's reflection to the letter – 'Death borders upon our birth, and our cradle stands in the grave.' These words remind me of my first visit to Shakespeare's tomb when I was told off by the verger for 'hurring' on the brass – the altar-rail. I was actually lost in wonder, thinking of the great poet buried seventeen feet down – they say – and under a good curse, so that nobody ever dared to dig him up and throw him into the bone-hole. The verger said he came from near Wormingford. 'Oh, what brought you here? Why did you leave?' 'My wife couldn't stand the way the brambles hung out of the hedges.' I hope Dogberry was listening.

The AGM

Two preoccupying matters this week are the severe frosts and the annual general meetings of all three PCCs. There is nothing to prove that the plum and pear blossom won't set, or that we shall reach 'Any other Business' without bloodshed.

Acts 6 could be said to be the inaugural chapter of the PCC. It was when the disciples complained that they could not be expected to preach the Gospel *and* wait on tables. Thus was our church administration born. Then a deacon, Stephen, proved that one could – and should. Stephen found that he could preach (brilliantly) and help cope with the practicalities of feeding and housing hundreds of converts who had given everything they owned to the Church and depended upon it for their very existence. Deaconatal headaches. Rows, quarrellings. But in our PCCs we all know our place and thank God for the worshipping accountant, electrician, cake-maker, those who can turn their hands to anything, and do. There is not much in the benefice which has to be farmed out. But high drama, of course, at the elections. Then we have those who want to come off the PCC on the flimsy excuse that they are now eighty, etc. Mrs X complains that it has worn her to the bone – a fib. Her bones are far from visible. To be honest, the elections are less to do with democracy than with ability. Mr X has served for ever, but who could, or would, do what he does? Treasurers are above rubies. Then there are those who never utter and who are advised when they have to put up their hands. Any other business can upset all the business which preceded it on the agenda. There is an indrawing of breath at the Quota, and another sound when Christian highmindedness has to be flattened by village common sense. Although it is ages since we had a real tussle, battles long ago echo in our subconscious. Generally speaking, though, our deliberations are reasonably if powerfully argued.

The three AGM venues are not without influence. Little Horkesley's and Mount Bures's are in Victorian schools which have become village halls, and Wormingford's takes place in the Cricket Pavilion. At Little Horkesley there is a pound-in-the-slot meter which sets off a warm, pentecostal gale which makes one speak up. At Mount Bures the official 1870 windows are purpose-built high enough to stop the farmworkers' children looking out, and thus day-dreaming, the great crime. At Wormingford, cricketers tiptoe between us with sorries and pardons and excuse mes, looking for this or that. Our respective clerks put it all down. Beside St Stephen, those who took part in the Church's first AGM were Philip, Prochorus, Nicanor, Timon, Parmenas and Nicolas, deacons all.

Rites of Passage

So much rural ministry is the unconscious or non-deliberate awakening of what is residual. A phrase, a tune, a word will do it. So this must mean that what is left and what remains – exists. A strong fact. Not much good and a great deal of harm can be the result of too much probing for what exists by way of belief when people apply for a rites of passage ceremony. Discovering what exists cannot be a matter of spiritual acupuncture, of trying to find the nerve. Bunyan almost went mad trying to find his and in the end it was the sensible Mrs Bunyan who hit upon Hebrews 12: 22–24 as the answer to her husband's terrible conviction that he had committed a sin which was not in the book, and for which, therefore, there was no forgiveness.

It has been a chilly St Mark's tide with the oaks coming before the ash. The Gospel is arrow-straight and swift, and its symbol is the lion-like creature from Ezekiel's dream which went directly forward. 'Where the spirit was to go, it went.' Looking at our three congregations, there is no knowing where the spirit has to go. I can see in some dear faces where it has *gone*, where it *is*. But strangers arrive to worship and what are their face values? Not for me to ask or assess. These strangers are journeying through life and now and then they pause to request one or other of the ceremonies of passage. Two have been asking for marriage. One who is old and dead is asking for cremation. Two are nine weeks of age and what they are asking is for a little less singing so that they can get to sleep. All will receive the Church's necessary words and acts as it touches what is residual in them of the faith, and perhaps causing it to grow.

'I publish the banns of marriage between . . . both of this parish.' And usually both of the same address. The girl will wear white, not to flout convention but because living with the boy carries with it no sense of impurity. He is clearly staggered when she arrives in white and each is obviously touched by the directness of the language. Something from it will always reside in them and can be added to later. On another occasion Godparents read alarming duties from huge cards. Like Bertha in Keats's *Eve of St Mark* they stare at 'a thousand things, the stars of heaven, and angels' wings' and think, 'how nice'.

May Day

'All good farmers go to Church' is among our wittier ads – meaning of course Mr Church our seed-merchant. Jennie Church sometimes plays for me at Mount Bures on an organ which John, who works in the great seed sheds, pumped by hand as a boy. I knew the triumphs and hazards myself. One could be thinking of something very interesting, and there would be no music. He and I go to the seed sheds to see a pollen mill, myself in a state of disbelief. A *pollen* mill? It is a very special mill of which he is the miller and it grinds pollen imported from China. There was the silk-route and now there is the pollen-route, and the latter ends at High Fen, which I can see through a haze of bare trees from the garden. John shows me a small packet and we muse on the countless Chinese bees and the thousands of Chinese flowers which went into it, so to speak. Outside is a much-loved lane of my childhood, a helter-skelter of a road which rushes one through a water-splash. This was the way to the bluebell woods and blackberrying. How strange if the pollen from our Arger Fen bees sped to the pollen mills of Beijing.

We roam from dusty seed-temple to seed-temple. No windows, otherwise they would be aviaries, and softly lit panels to catch the moths. The separator for peas is the same as that used for diamonds. A revolving drum lined with gramophone needles picks out the peas with weevil holes. John and I climb ladders, walk planks, journey through soft canyons of hessian and are in the realm of embryo, whilst on the other side of the wall every wild and cultivated plant heads for its maturity. I tell John how our local pilgrim fathers, hundreds of them, took their Suffolk and Essex seed-corn with them when they sailed to Massachusetts. And, having no sorting drums with gramophone needles, took lots of our wildflowers too. What a comfort to find some Arger Fen bluebells blooming in embryonic Boston. John said that one of his duties was to maintain the true vetch for our county. We emerged via cracked mustard, kibbled mace, salad rape, coriander, and sacks of exquisite linseed, each seed a polished jewel, to cold sunlight.

It was an American, Charles Warner, a friend of Mark Twain, who wrote, 'To own a bit of ground, to scratch it with a hoe, to plant seeds, and watch the renewal of life – this is the commonest delight of the race, the most satisfactory thing a man can do.' One can only hope that what one seeds will 'come true'. Like our vetch. Crop trials are held in the fields surrounding the great sheds in which the seeds find their perfection. Listening my way round the parishes, I find myself in a new country the moment someone draws me into the secrets of his work – John, for instance. His seedsman's philosophy has altered my geography.

Meekly Kneeling

We have been gallivanting around in cowslip-land, the string of Suffolk villages north of Long Melford, and sure enough there they were all in bloom on the roadside, the peggles of childhood. Also a stupendous showing of blackthorn. Hartest church with its snowy interior, plus memories of devout picnics in farmer Hunnable's barn. Then across the cold fields to St Petronilla's, Whepstead. Some say that this first-century lady was St Peter's daughter. The syllables of her name chime in the landscape. Then to handsome Denston which is so wondrously carved with 'affronted' beasts, hounds, harts, hares, lions, a crane, that it could be dedicated to David Attenborough. It always pleases me to see how much of nature manages to get into a church.

Back home the Flower Festival begins to raise its demanding head. I missed it last time, being in Scotland, but am gradually being forgiven. This year's theme is Kneelers. When did hassocks go out and kneelers come in? Hassocks came in all heights and were often amazingly heavy. Saintly folk with creaking joints lugged them into their pews by their furry ears. They tended to smell like small animals and were stuffed so tight with straw that a lifetime's prayer barely dented them. But now – kneelers. Embroidered works of art, and no two alike. Kneeling has a chequered history. In our three churches we are all *genuflectentes* ('those who kneel') and are not standers or crouchers. I am often touched by the way in which young and old seem to fall into Tudor attitudes at the altar-rail. It was not always so. George Herbert had to teach his Bemerton flock to kneel and Jane Austen's brother was known as 'the officer who knelt in church' – being the only one to do so. Before hassocks went out and kneelers came in, I used to balance on a coconut-matting stool which marked me with small ridges. Now we sink in heraldry, botany, into Auriol and Pip's masterpieces.

Christ, Stephen, Peter and Paul, each kneel down but once in the New Testament, the Lord in the garden of Gethsemane, Stephen in the stoning-pit, Peter before raising Dorcas the needlewoman from the dead, and Paul before setting out to Jerusalem, where he thought he would be killed. So at the beginning kneeling was when one was *in extremis*, in danger, in acceptance of God's will.

The liturgy allows us – or demands of us – an interesting variety of kneeling. 'All kneeling', 'still kneeling', 'kneeling humbly', 'meekly kneeling', etc. Down we go on to a million fine stitches and the inspiration of the Royal School of Needle-work. A few folk cling to their family hassocks and the cosy whiff of mice. In one sanctuary I kneel on marble and it is not unpleasant.

Easter Four: St Philip and St James

B arrie having won a Trip to Cambridge in a raffle, off we go, five ringers in one car, myself the honorary ringer and eventual guide. Do I start earning my keep on the way or when we get there? The conversation is too arresting to interrupt, these belfry friends having known each other for ever, as the saying goes. Thus we carry our parochiality with us and I constrain myself from pointing to the sights *en route* so that I can listen to the weaving in and out of bell-talk. There is where Captain Oates of self-sacrificing memory lived. There is the Yeldham oak, under which St Cedd preached the Gospel. 'There are some nice sheep by the side of the road,' says Meriel. The day threatens splendour. There are cuckoos, cowslips in ditches, and little traffic on the B-roads. But here is Cambridge and I can start. Our itinerary is Great St Mary's, King's, of course, the Backs, a good pub, and the Botanical Gardens. The tourists haven't quite arrived and the lovely golden-grey heart of the place has yet to be impacted by a million others doing what we are doing now. The chestnuts and willows are in mint condition, and the lawns are deliciously fresh. I feel happily reformed in St Mary's. I can catch the distant voices of Erasmus, Herbert, Latimer, Cranmer, all lecturing. We discover that the

pulpit is movable and that Barrie has rung the bells. He has rung the bells of England.

Buying tickets for King's Chapel, we are gently asked if we are English. 'What are we to say to that?' says someone. The amazing building is a kind of housed rainbow, scientifically weighted, yet gossamer. Meriel stands before the great east window a long time, then says, 'That's how it was – turmoil!' wild, cruel crowds hurrying that poor young man to His death, like those whipped-up fundamentalist mobs one sees on television. Nothing has changed. She observes that in so many pictures and windows of the Crucifixion how it is all so neat, with few present except the principal characters. They – the crowds – were there all right. Read all four gospels. He died amid uproar. Religious multitudes – the nastiest noise in the world. A score or so children are being taught fan-vaulting; their brilliant eyes wander aloft.

The Botanical Gardens are, for me the guide, what they call

an unqualified success. I think of my dear old late friend S. D. Garrett, who years ago, used to lend me his Fellow's key to let myself in. I want to pat the immense trees and have a word here and there with those plants which he used to show me. Then back home in the evening light, Barrie, Mary, Meriel and Dorothy, for the ringing practice, and myself to weed.

Dame Julian

U P early to give the annual Julian Lecture at Norwich. The familiar road is not as they said it would be on the news, jammed with VE Day traffic. In fact it is strangely empty, but exceedingly hot. Glazed Norfolk pantiles and flinty cottages sparkle in the sun, and rape flowers fiercely on the great East Anglian plain. Entering Norwich, I take a particular note of the shrubbed gardens in the residential streets which, in May, deserve to be placed among the glories of England, although precious little mention is made of them in the guidebooks. It takes the French – Colette, Alain-Fournier – to grow rapturous at the sight of lilacs, horse-chestnuts and wistarias topping secretive walls and bursting through wrought-iron gates. Blooming suburbs indeed.

St Julian's, like our church at Little Horkesley, is a phoenix risen from the ashes. Both were obliterated by German bombs during the last war, their millennial quiet all gone in a second. Each picked up the pieces and continued on its sacred way. Present, lots of Julian ladies, a few in habits, most in silks, some pilgrims, the Rural Dean, the expected sprinkling of friends, and the shrine itself, the latter uncluttered so as to leave space for our thoughts. Last year's lecturer wishes me good luck as though I was about to go on trial and could end up in the Lollards' pit. My chief anxiety is to keep my mind on my address when, as St John of the Cross and Thomas Traherne discovered, everything I see is so distractingly wonderful. Each of them eventually gave up, accepting that the distraction was the reality:

> So now if from this day
> I am not found among the haunts of men,
> Say that I went astray
> Love-stricken on my way.

Little resurrected St Julian's is bright and cool. Also heavy with eucharistic incense, and so not a bit like Little Horkesley. The first part of my lecture is a brief play which I wrote about Julian having tea with Evelyn Underhill, with 600 years between them, two clever women chatting about timelessness. From the corner of my eye I can see into the cell, and all the fragmentation made whole. Maybe he is still living – the young *Luftwaffe* man who aimed at a factory and dynamited a vision. They say that the population of Norwich in Julian's time was half made up of visionaries. If only they had all put pen to paper as a reclusive requirement. I spoke of desert-dwellers in cities, then and now. In Norwich the crowds began to move toward the celebration of 8 May 1945. Inside, we considered 8 May 1373, when a young woman stopped dying because she had a book to write.

VE Day: 8 May 1995

The sun has barely risen before it is beating down. A voice on *Prayer for the Day* says that we should find significance in all that we do. Quite so. I walk in the wet early morning grass to take a look at yesterday's toil, always the best part of gardening. I am looking for significance, and there it is. Paul told the Corinthians that 'There are, it may be, many kinds of voices in the world, and none of them is without signification.' This would seem to suggest a writer's ear. Living so remotely that village voices have to be carried to me on the wind, distant yells from the cricket ground, floating conversations of girls riding by, the regular Saturday rumble of three elderly brothers on their afternoon walk, when I do get out the overhearing of 'so many kinds of voices in the world' is fascinating. 'Do you get out much?' is a question I am often asked.

This week I appear to have been avoiding the significance of what everyone else has been up to. Thus, I can hardly believe it when, at crack of dawn, Basil arrives from Bures St Mary (not to be confused with Mount Bures or Bures Hamlet, and a more significant place altogether if numbers are the criterion) with a printed account of all that has occurred in this village since May 1945. He lists some twenty shops (there are now six), a jam factory, two blacksmiths and many other disappearances. Searching for significance, I recall old Mr M the grocer, who wore wigs as one would shirts, a change of colour each day, and I remember the riverside lanes down which on blazing-hot days a boy would be swallowed alive by cow-mumble and butterbur. Dwarfed by great weeds, I made wearying journeys to relations through scratchy jungles who were not always pleased to be disturbed. And then my offerings were not always welcome. A nice bunch of lilac for grandmother and, 'Take it out, take it out!' She would have crossed herself had she known the significance of this gesture. Then she would smooth my injured feelings. No, she did not know *why* lilac must not be brought into the house, but it must not. And that was that. Call it unlucky. These days, being not without courage, I always bring lilac into the house. I set it in a fat pot before the bread-oven. Should I find it knocked over, I will blame the cat. I shall also blame Keith Thomas's *Religion and the Decline of Magic*, and my passion for lilac perfume.

I unveil the VE Day memorial on Mount Bures green. At Wormingford we sing 'I vow to thee, my country' and I read Keith Douglas poems from the pulpit. Such anniversaries possess rituals which must not be broken but must be refurbished. People are so disappointed if we don't have this or that.

Easter Five

Up betimes. A long morning, indeed, a long day. The valley is summery and heady with may, lilac and rape. Matins at Wormingford, where I give a little lecture on Charles Wesley and the doctrinal nature of his hymns. Then a great weeding of the garden, a dreadful sheep and goats business, I fear, as I pull out some intruders but allow others – red campion, magnificent buttercups, stands of handsome white nettle – to hobnob with the roses. A hurried tea then to Little Cornard to preach at the Flower Festival. The deep lane up to the high church is that which I walked as a child with my mother, and which the youthful Thomas Gainsborough climbed to paint his 'Cornard Wood'. It is dense with Queen Anne's Lace (transferred from the Virgin or her mother St Anna? hazards Geoffrey Grigson).

I preach on the virtues of inattention, on the wandering eye of the child during service-time, which was my own wandering eye, of course. I admit to poring over the botanical illustrations and maps which came after Revelation in my schoolboy Bible as the sermon rolled on. I talk about that most interesting command to consider the lilies of the field – not just glance at them, but consider them. The Old Testament takes coriander into consideration. Day-dreams at Evensong. The pale faces of the congregation tilt towards mine. We are all locked in by scent and bloom, whilst the church itself is very near to being locked into a farmyard.

Having rashly offered to reorganize the Rogation for Little Horkesley, I am amazed by the time it takes. When George Herbert rightly declared that hurry was the death of prayer he might have added, 'and don't imagine that you will be able to compose enough new prayers for the Rogation walk in anything under a week.' So I make a prayer-map for the village, in case we lose our way on the home ground. We shall crocodile through its pastures and corn, past its stock and ponds, by its pub and cottages, in and out of its gardens and orchards, and to our graves, singing, reading, praying, remembering to ask, but not beating our bounds, which are miles away. How hard it is in today's countryside to retain the old relevance, to keep the Faith and not the theme-park. 'And I say unto you, "Ask",' they would say. I dare say that members of our perambulating church will be asking themselves what sense the set-aside as they rogate next Sunday. Let's hope it doesn't rain, although we shall be asking it to, only in due season, that is later on in the afternoon.

St Matthias

It is a truth universally acknowledged that a country writer in possession of a public must be in want of 'characters'. 'I know some real characters,' Edward tells me, the implication being that they are now few and far on the ground and that I need someone like him to guide me to their haunts. He himself is a character, of course, but modesty forbids him to admit it. Characters may only be discovered among the 'old people' – i.e. indigenous villagers of all ages who just happen to go on doing things in the old way, or thinking in the old way, or just looking in the old way. Although often a trial, they are greatly respected. Generally, one has to be over forty at least to be a character. Characters under twenty-five are known as nuisances. As for characters in the making, well let John Keats describe adolescence: 'There is a space of life between [boy and man], in which the soul is in ferment, the character undecided, the way of life uncertain, the ambition thick-sighted . . .' If we live long enough we all become characters of sorts, especially people who can't drive a car, use a computer and who write books at the end of a track. Edward thinks that the character I should meet would best be trapped round about teatime, when she would be least likely to bolt at our knock. I have to explain that I do not have to stalk this character as I might the badgers at dusk, as I have known her for ages. Gloom descends on him. 'What'll we do when she's gone? When they've all gone? The characters.' Have a bit of peace, I was going to say, but instead I found myself explaining how the writer saw the extraordinary in the ordinary, and how little was the 'normal' normal to him. 'You're a character all right,' I could see him thinking.

It is St Matthias-tide. What would I not give to know his

characteristics. Twelfth-man, and that by lottery, he appears in the Gospels like one of those outline figures which we had to fill in with our own colours when we were small. Both he and the more revealingly named Judas Barsabbas were found fit to complete the sacred circle which had been fractured by Judas. There are hazy recollections of a Gospel according to St Matthias, but it got lost like our own East Anglian Gospel-book which St Felix carried ashore here in the seventh century. M. R. James – now there's a character, if you like – said that it may have been cut up for game-labels by a Victorian squire. Watching the Great Fire of London, Pepys said, 'Oh, the books, all the books . . .' A number of villagers I have known achieved character status simply by 'reading his (or her) life away'. The postman would find them at it before eight in the morning. Reading books. What characters, if not much use.

St Dunstan

I am having my eyes tested, and not before time. The first test is a yellow brick road which runs to infinity. But then the tester changes such a crystal-clear path and makes it impossible for me to see where I am going. 'Good,' she says. Little air-puffs are directed against each pupil. 'Good,' she says. I am followed by a teenager whose road peters out (he says) and does not run to infinity. Good. Then in to an optician who performs magic with discs and diminishing letters. This time I am more than just good, I am remarkable. He invites a colleague to stare at this remarkable me. 'You have young eyes!' They beam. No disease, no strain in spite of having several million pages of print passed before them; no, I am untouched by wear and tear. As good as new. The optician brings the conversation round to his uncle, Canon Dobree, and his work on medieval wall paintings. An exquisite Crucifixion has been found under the whitewash of ages in Brent Eleigh church, a masterpiece by a Suffolk Giotto. The presence of such pictures under the limewash can often be sensed before they are revealed, rather like truffles under the woodland mould. They *fade* into view – eventually – having once been whitened out of sight. They are a kind of cataract art. The 'poor man's Bible', thought to have been superseded by the printing-press, glimmers down to the kneeler at the altar, pale, visionary, very beautiful, telling of centuries of eyes lifted up to it.

It was once quite common to be part-blind half one's life. Nothing could be done about it. Samuel Pepys had to abandon his diary and most of his reading because his eyes began to pain him when he was still in his mid-thirties. A few years earlier he had himself fired one of the guns which welcomed home King Charles II – 'But holding my head too much over the gun, I have almost spoiled my right eye.' His contemporary, John Milton, told a friend:

> This three years' day these eyes, though clear
> To outward view, of blemish or of spot;
> Bereft of light their seeing hath forgot . . .

There is a poignant description of seeking enlightenment in Isaiah. 'We grope for the wall like the blind, and we grope as if we had no eyes, we stumble at noon day as in the night . . .' 'O dark, dark, dark, amid the blaze of noon, irrecoverably dark . . .' cries Milton's Samson. Only a sightless man could have written this poem. Blindness in the Lord's Palestine was endemic. 'How were your eyes opened?' demanded the authorities. By some kind of charlatanry is what they are getting at.

Angered by their insinuation the man who had been cured by Christ bursts out, 'One thing I know, that whereas I was blind, now I can see!'

The Baptism of Lukas

The decks are cleared, although this is hardly the right word, for the baptism of Lukas. There is frost in the air and all the birds are singing. Lukas lives at Crabbes Farm and will at this very moment be lying beside his golden christening robe, his gold medallion from Constantinople and other reminders of where he comes from. Not only 'From God, who is our home', but from mighty rifts and schisms. Thus, when the bells fall silent and matins begin, and I peer into the full nave, I see what history does to us all; gives us among other things different and distinctive – and beautiful – religious cultures. Lukas's is part Greek Orthodox, part Huguenot and part solid East Anglian, and here are all his relations to prove it. The child of Vicky and Trevor joins the children of Byzantium, of Luther and Calvin, of Cranmer and the Wesleys. Here we all are clutching large baptismal cards (series two), whilst Meriel the organist boils a kettle of hot water in the vestry to take the chill off the font, Paul the priest hunts around for a purificator, and I think of how I am to link the Little Horkesleyians with the elegant Athenians in the address. We don't have Athenians in the congregation every day, although there is always a fair smattering, did we take the trouble to note it, of Scottish dissenters and refugees from recent Anglican practices, and a Quaker or two.

Lukas arrives. He is four months old and serene. The silk fringe of his ancient robe is entangled with his mother's ornaments when the moment comes for her to hand him over to Paul and they have to be separated all over again. The youthful godparents promise the earth and the tragic cattle can be heard across the meadows. Lukas remains silent except for a tiny gasp of surprise as the water splashes his brow. We sing Moultrie's fine translation from the Liturgy of St James, 'Let all mortal flesh keep silence'. This very latest scrap of mortal flesh obeys the hymn to the letter. His perfect face is still, yet wide awake. The Athenians and the Huguenots and the East Anglians sing 'Rank on rank the host of heaven spreads its vanguard on the way' whilst smiling at him out of the corners of their eyes.

Then we all go to the Crabbes Farm barn for wine and fruit salad and christening cake, as big a party of heretics and schismatics as one could find outside a history book. But dear Christian souls withal. The quiet boy lies decked in Orthodox gold among his presents, a violin, miniature furniture, his borrowed robe, the bound copy of his family tree. I talk to the Greek ladies about Suffolk and pause to say hello to the heifers as we leave. They respond with their customary innocence and delight.

Rogation

Rogation at Little Horkesley. Lots of children and all of us. We walk, a robed choir and stoutly shod congregation through the 'lands, meadows, pastures, groves, streams, tithes, and all their things' which in AD 1115 Robert and Beatrice Godebold gave to Cluny. But here they all remain, more or less, and are now in the possession of us 'asking' tramps. The delicious May air and our songs mingle as we follow the itinerary. The swallows glide, the horse-pond glints weedily. John Copsey's beasts lift their heavy heads to take stock of us and exchange looks with their trusting eyes, observing our prayerful crocodile. Advice and beseechings from the farmers of Judaea echo in the Sunday quiet. Unaccompanied hymns rise with a full unexpected sweetness from the shining fields, puzzling the cuckoo and, in my dream, joining Cluniac voices. We ask, I fear, for what we know Anglia Water and the European Community's Common Agricultural Policy are obliged to give us. Yet on a day like this the ancient sacredness of the village stares through its current economy like palimpsest, and we certainly do not feel that we are engaged in some picturesque irrelevance. Quite the opposite. For one thing the rogatory language has an earthiness which includes us as well as the crops, the trees, and especially the grass, that image of the temporary. Have no doubt about it, we are asking for nothing less than our lives. Thus we end up in the churchyard, having done the growing rounds, Micky's apple trees, John's wheat and beet, Kate's borders, Constable's river, and all our boundaries and horizons. I read from imploring psalms about walking in vain shadows and being a stranger and sojourner even in this home spot. Old Mrs Munson, landlady of the Beehive, lies at my feet under a mountain of wreaths. Last week her dust joined that

of the Cluniac monks. *Domine, refugium* indeed. The children's eyes are still bright from conversations with calves and pigs.

Then a visit to the much maligned suburbs of surrounding towns, which at this moment just ask to be seen. Blossom hangs from a thousand walls and drifts through a thousand gates. The eighteen-year-old Alain-Fournier who would write a single masterpiece, *Le Grand Meaulnes*, before the Western Front finished him, wrote of the London suburbs, 'windows of coloured glass and lace curtains. Foliage everywhere, the notes of a piano and flute rising up on every side.' All this in 1905.

Meditation

They say meditation is novice work and not to be compared with contemplation. Child's stuff. But it is as far as I have got. 'In meditation we converse with ourselves; in prayer we converse with God,' said Matthew Henry. As a nonconformist with a great way with words, he would not have been easy with non-discursive mental prayer. To discover a contemplative at work in a village church in England makes one faintly uneasy. Not to find one in a French or Russian church is unusual; some Anna-like face in the shadows, some kneeling man staring straight ahead. What I find as I enter His gates with praise for Nikolaus Pevsner are countrywomen hard at work with Brasso and secateurs conversing with each other. I must also confess that the notice on the medieval door, written in a fine calligraphic hand, gently reminding me where I am and what to do – kneel, of course – receives no more than a nod. But sometimes when the flower-ladies are not there, so as to avoid consternation, I take a few first steps towards contemplation, meekly kneeling upon my knees and savouring the stored-up quietness. The clock in the tower clunks and rumbles, the tree which will have to be cut back scratches the window. The question is, when – at what moment – did I stop talking to myself and start talking to Christ? Who can tell? What a long way I have to go before I catch up with those still figures who drop in for a word with God on their way to the butcher in Bonneval or the office in Caracas.

'Do you meditate?' asked a friend. She did for twenty minutes every morning. She put aside every other thought to think of God. I confessed to being less disciplined. Then I realized that, living as I do in the middle of nowhere, as it is described in the village, many of my days were helplessly meditative from

waking to sleeping, though broken into by work. I wished I could have retorted as a boy that I wasn't day-dreaming, a crime which would lead straight to the dole queue, but Meditating. People must meditate on whether they have what it takes to contemplate. Nor do matters end there. Having 'acquired' contemplation, one can go on and on, like those academically enslaved creatures who journey all their lives towards the ultimate thesis. Can they overtake the prayer-filled faces of the simple regulars in the nave?

The pre-service vestry I find intensely meditative. Waiting for the introit to die away, the bell to halt. Robed and still among the clutter, every minute private and precious, as against the different preciousness of the corporate hour and the rows of familiar heads whose prayer-progress will remain a mystery.

Matins

May dawns are too special to be missed and the early hours are a holiday in themselves. I recall my father's passion for them. Wraith-like water-meadows around Garnon's, the crops still holding on to yesterday's sunshine, the chaotic birdsong, the immense ramparts of may blossom sheltering Chagall-like ponies, and Max dancing about in the wet grass, trying to kid me that he has just seen-off a sabre-toothed tiger or at least Bart's dog. This all at six o'clock, which for my father would have been a bit late in the day. 'Do you call this *morning*?'

I have been reading of old King David, now on his deathbed, 'the sweet psalmist of Israel', and of his telling his son Solomon

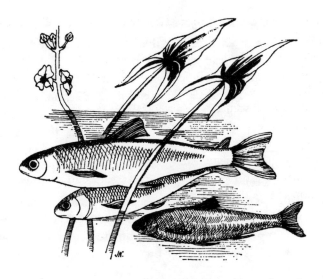

that a ruler must be 'as the light of the morning when the sun rises, even a morning without clouds' and like clear shining grass after rain. Like an English May dawn, in fact. Was Reginald Heber, still in his twenties, thinking of this dayspring king when he wrote, 'Brightest and best of the sons of the morning' for the Epiphany? 'Like some tall palm the noiseless fabric sprang' was how he had once described the building of the Temple in a poem whose eastern-jewel note might well have recommended this young Yorkshire clergyman for translation to Calcutta. Heber's spicy imagery filled my head as I stared across the river to crack-of-dawn Wissington, where it often looks oriental in the white mists.

'Have you a favourite hymn?' I asked Rosa, who was singing in the choir seventy years ago and whose meticulous settings of the liturgy lie on the choirstalls every Sunday without fail. 'Through all the changing scenes of life' she replied without hesitation. David's psalm rhymed by Tate and Brady and written by him when he was young and frightened. It was then that he saw that those who looked to God for protection 'lightened'.

We, to be honest, have been darkened by sickness. 'What can you expect? – it is our age.' True enough, though darkening all the same. How good they are to each other during this darkening. All the practical help, all the common sense, the visiting, the shopping, the keeping in mind, the treks to the General Hospital. Some vanish with alarming speed, others hang on to their earthly existence. My old friend the artist John Nash, casting a caustic eye on the morning's obituaries, used to mutter, 'Old So-and-So – falling off the perch – what a fool!' The old know what it was like to have been the sons and daughters of the morning.

Rogation Two

Retaining the social realism of the old agricultural community and making it relevant in today's terms is a constant battle. Ours is a short walk compared with those earlier marathons which took the whole village to its bounds, first to show the boys where they were, then to see if Great Horkesley had encroached upon them, worse, to shift them, the latter deserving the curse of Deuteronomy 27:17. I suspect that I am the only person on this annual trudge who knows where some of the Little Horkesley landmarks are. Just down the road from the Beehive Inn, dense with spring growth, lie the boundaries of a Celtic settlement. And just below my garden there yawns an alarmingly deep ditch which for a thousand years or more has marked the beginning of Wormingford.

After a brief but fierce ecological talk by me, we all set out for green pastures, for cornfields, for the old horse-pond (all those generations of ploughing beasts drawing up gallons of water with gulps and snorts, their reins hanging loose at the close of day), for the farm, for Kate's vegetables and orchard, her children up the trees, and eventually for the churchyard, where we must all end. Then back to life inside the church with 'Thine be the Glory' and a ragged procession under the scaffolding. A new blue ceiling. Our old churches took so long to build that many people would not have known what it was like to worship without scaffolding. I can hear friends at Westminster Abbey saying, 'What's new!' Once at St Mary's Bury St Edmund's I saw a Stanley Spencer painting being modelled overhead. Forty-two carved angels and martyrs from the fifteenth century, and a dozen young roofers from the twentieth century, plus radios, of course, all swinging aloft. The Temple was built in silence. How? But back to our asking journey among the crops, and to the strangely beseeching nature of Christ's 'Ask'.

This has always moved me. 'Ask for the old paths, the good way,' implores Jeremiah of half-lost Israel. The Lord is reproachful. 'So far you have asked nothing in my name: *ask* and you will receive.' Our farm and field asking lacks the old intensity. Local agriculture supplies but a fraction of the local needs. And there is always Sainsbury's. What is silently being asked during this crocodile Rogation as it weaves its way to the growing-places is that some of us will be made well again. Health-wise it has been a bad year. On the positive side, nobody has needed to ask for help when they wanted it most.

Ascension

With the may bushes and the cow parsley clearly never having heard of such things as the sumptuary laws, I wander through their heady foam to the church. I am urged to 'fervent charity' and to speak 'as the oracles of God'. Apart from uproar in the school playground, there are no other voices, no ring or clink of men at work, not even the clipped repartee of some thirties' movie in the afternoon slot to suggest that my neighbours have their feet up. Stillness is all. Back on my desk lies the Census Return for the village in 1871 from which I learn that William Ward (30), his wife Mary (42) and their ploughman Charles Mingey (18) lived in my house. The brick floors still dip from their scrubbings and hobnails – from where 'the dead feet walked in' as Hardy put it. I learn too from the Census of that poor, companionable army of labourers and lads which even in May would have been slogging or 'tifling about' or singing or calling on our dozen or so farms. And of a similar host of servants and governesses, horsemen (not to be confused with labourers), bailiffs, needlewomen, blacksmiths and millers, all drowning in the voluptuary whiteness. I remember Hoo, for me the loveliest of all field-churches, where at Whitsun only the tips of the tombs could be seen dipping like grey boats on an ocean of Queen Anne's Lace. I had an old farmworker friend there who read the lesson. When it carried him away, as it often did, he would pause then say, 'That was very fine. I'll read that agen.' The immeasurability of faith, of belief, of the effect of language on an acute ear. This aged ploughman delighted in Harriet Auber's 'Comforter who came/ Sweet influence to impart'. He would have been perplexed had he known that I still hear him in my head as one of the oracles of God.

Toil is so discreet in today's countryside where most of the hard work goes into leisure. What must be done is done when no one is looking. Or so it seems. Philip has renewed all the stiles. Bernard has mown the green lane into a green highway. All the acres are as neat as a pin. Yet not a soul about. Scent from a million bluebells at Arger Fen drifts lazily across the beet and I can see the long nude stalks trailing from my bicycle long ago. I can also see the small boy having to fetch mumble (the matchless cow-parsley) for my pet rabbits. Someone is arriving to fetch ivy from near my brook for a wedding, huge plastic bags of it. It pulls up dank and glossy, and seemingly astonished at being chosen.

Vézèlay

It happens every now and then that one cannot be where one should be. Engagement blocks the way. But how am I to explain this to the neighbours? 'Where were *you* on Thursday?' I could have said, 'In Vézèlay for the Ascension' – a young man on his first visit to France. For I have always drawn on a memory-bank of past festivals when for some excellent reason or other I cannot make the one being celebrated in our village. It was in Vézèlay that I first had some comprehension of that 'cloud of unknowing' which hides the total Christ from my earth-limited gaze. When I woke up there on that bright morning I had quite forgotten that it was Ascension Day and I had to ask what was going on. They were shining the stairs at the hotel, watering the pavement and hurrying to and fro. Even the house martins were extra shrill. The steep street up to the great basilica was in tumult. Crashing continental bells without a tune to their name, pushing crowds, happy old nuns in knitted shawls and everyone and everything going up, up, up. Except Henry Rushbury, an elderly English RA, who held his ground and sat at his easel drawing architecture, and let the Ascension roar round him. But what was going on? Why, *l'Ascension*! *l'Ascension*! 'So may we also in heart and mind thither ascend, and with Him continually dwell.' Indeed.

Looking up my impressions of this tremendous day I read, 'The buildings themselves seem to jostle for a footing on the cobbled slope. Palaces and patisseries are hugger-mugger. Garden gates just manage to hold back lilacs and wistarias which are fighting to get out. Patches of hot sun and then black shadows where the dogs pant. I read each passing plaque; Romain Rolland lived here (what a nice house; just right for a novelist), *Le Maison de Théodore de Bèze* (Calvin's friend); Camille Desmoulins, 19, *Mort pour la Résistance*. Poor Camille, a little younger than myself. May he with Him continually dwell. Many windows are flung wide so that I can take stock of interiors. Many scrubbed tables and a pale, stale essence of countless meals. I can also smell fresh milk and bread and byres and cake. Up we all go, pressing on to the basilica. There is no going back. Soon the marvellous church speaks with such a mighty voice as to subdue our holiday voices. It is very near now. The shops are full of saints and tin pagodas spin views of Burgundy and holy people around.

At last we are there, and I am suddenly on my own in the narthex and then an insect in a Romanesque forest. The organist, I am informed, is playing Stravinsky. *Stravinsky?* 'Where were you last Thursday?' 'Oh, I was at *l'Ascension* in Vézèlay, seeing the Lord in his whirling clothes and with his huge hand palm-outward.'

Sunday After the Ascension

The School Governors' meeting. Where would we be without Mr Davis to guide us through the labyrinthine agenda? The lavish bureaucracy of the 1993 Education Act spreads before us. Undaunted, brave as lions, we handle vast sums, decree this and that in the voice of experts. Should we stray, the kind headmaster brings us back to the balance-sheet. Above the false ceiling soars the churchy gothic of the Victorian building in which two girls, Miss Jane Newman aged nineteen and Miss Fanny Nears aged fourteen, taught some seventy 'scholars' according to the requirements of the 1870 Education Act. Their scholars were all under twelve. Rows of Arthurs and Emmas, banks of Georges and Marys, the Bones brothers, Jonathan, Ephraim and Alfred, and three 'Henerys' [sic]. Their sons will sail to Gallipoli. Their grown-up brothers and sisters, nearly a hundred of them aged thirteen and over, will toil on the farms and in service. Below the school, in the vicarage which continues to glow between the trees, dwelt Mr Tufnell the vicar, his wife and their cook, housemaid, kitchen-maid, coachman and groom. I nod to them familiarly, having just encountered them in the Census. I hear them lifting the varnished roof with, 'What is the meaning of Empire-day? Why do the cannons roar . . . ?'

Christopher Woods, our Rural Dean, held an Ascension Day service in the school surrounded by art-work. All the children here are at the genius stage in painting. Alas, as Wordsworth implies, this must fade for them as for the rest of us, for if the inconvenience of inspiration isn't held in check by common sense, where would we all be? The children have their eyes on our north aisle as a picture-gallery. Their forerunners filled their slates with coloured chalks, then washed their art away to make a space for arithmetic. Those Bones boys, they lie under the cedars. Those Henerys, they sang in the choir on Sunday nights. What did these scholars learn? Little that we can now comprehend.

We have two classes. Eleven children are in the first, thirteen in the second. They arrive in cars and buses and begin to shout the minute they pass the gate. In the modified Victorian edifice which still shows a certain sharp progressive pride, the children are conversational, with cheek prophesying wit. We governors are their slaves, working away at all hours to give them what they expect and, myself, ever fearful of the County Council whacking me over the knuckles for day-dreaming.

Thomas Traherne

C. S. Lewis once described Traherne's *Centuries* as 'almost the most beautiful thing in English literature'. Certainly, this marvellous book comes very near to being the happiest thing in English Christianity. After my lecture at the Traherne Festival a young man, who was about the same age as the poet when he wrote *Centuries*, stood up to ask, simply, 'how could he?' How could he be so joyfully affirmative when he must have witnessed Civil War horrors of Bosnian ghastliness? Well, how could he? I had no answer. We were in Credenhill church on the eve of Trinity Sunday, a place which with Little Gidding and Bemerton is part of a wonderful triune Anglican 'intelligence'. The church stands high up above the Wye and it was filled with those who, like myself, require their saints to be wordsmiths. The forging of *Centuries*, and the priest–poet's other writings, was certainly miraculous. Thomas Traherne was hungry, ravenous, for joy, but for fame he appeared to have no appetite at all. He begs all kinds of questions. How, for instance, could such a glorious writer be content to write for just one pair of eyes – those of a Mrs Hopton, who had temporarily slipped into popery, and who had to be re-confirmed in Anglicanism via his ecstatic and unique language? But then we haven't much to go on in this direction. My young questioner hazarded that celebrated passages such as 'The Corn was Orient and Immortal Wheat' was in effect an elegy on the lovely Hereford of Traherne's childhood which the bloody fighting and mayhem of the 1640s had ruined.

I felt overwhelmed to be reading Traherne's writings in the church where his voice had sounded. Mine and the other scholars' papers failed to explain him. Nor could we bring him to the real attention of those listening to us, for his is that form of happiness which travels at the speed of light, and is well on its way in a single spoken sentence from his work. When Richard Birt inspired these Trinity gatherings at Credenhill five years ago, his purpose was partly to re-establish the claims of happiness and delight as being a necessary aspect of the Christian experience. Traherne's is the ultimate apology for such claims.

Outside, thin skeins of summer rain blurred the Black Mountains. The park trees were drenched and shadowy, and the steep path up which Traherne climbed to his matins was wet and glittering. 'When I came into the Country, and being seated among silent Trees, and had all my Time in my own Hands, I resolved to spend it all, whatever it cost me, in Search of Happiness.' He did not have to search far.

Trinity Sunday: the Flower Festival

The flower festival is upon us. Blessed Gertrude, Constance, Anna, have mercy. Tantalizing weather blows cold then hot, teacups rattle on the tombs, cuckoos call from Arger Fen, rooks debate in Philip's new-mown hay, commanding women cry 'Oasis! Stepladder! Leaves, more leaves'. Husbands are in need of special prayers. There are charming tents under the trees, garlanded perpendicular, an alabaster St Alban under a pergola, artful drifts of roses, our de-wormed Victorian hearse burdened with lilies, our font a pool of infant buds. The carboy is full of pounds (thank Heaven); and Harold's honey-bees, weighed down with loot, hum against the sanctuary window (1866) in which Mary, with a halo, listens, and Martha, without a halo, carries a huge pile of washing-up. There is intensive child labour – 'Fetch me some more water and see that you don't spill it' – and then comes the immortal moment, the flinging open to the world of our south door, the oohs and ahs, the wonder. Did we ever see anything like it? Only once a year. Billy and Pat, whose last Festival this is, beam modestly. O prosper thou our handy-work. Amen say their obedient husbands, dreaming of whisky.

In the evening I conduct the now immensely popular hymn-fest, standing in the pulpit like a jack-in-the-box. The village has chosen its ten favourite hymns, writing them on the church door like Luther's ninety-five theses. The church is crowded and I stare down on the myriad countenances of friends and flowers. To space our songs I give miniature talks on the words and the music, and everybody falls back into their seats with unconcealed self-indulgence. The publicly singing individual is never more privately devout. Fine poetry, adequate rhyme, adored tunes, confident doctrine, up it all soars. Who is to evaluate it? No one. Did they know that their beloved 'Dear Lord and Father of Mankind' is the last part of a poem called 'The brewing of Soma' in which Whittier denounces an ecstasy drink used in vedic worship? Of course not, but what's new? At the moment, everything. Parry, Bunyan, Canon Dearmer, the enchanting Bianco, Sir Henry Baker, Bishop Heber, Mr Chalmers-Smith from Scotland, St Clement, John Marriott, who as well as writing 'Thou, whose almighty word' composed 'Marriage is like a Devonshire Lane', all are new. Our children ring Cowper on silver hand-bells. Worn out, we wander home.

Corpus Christi

Home after Loch Rannoch wanderings. It was during his absenteeism at this time of the year that John Wesley defended himself with the famous excuse of 'I look upon all the world as my parish.' His meddling in other men's parishes at that moment had been in Somerset, where the childlike, artless love of the local people had enchanted him. So different from his querulous Londoners. In a letter containing this excuse he had reminded a friend that there was no place in all the world, Christian or otherwise, which was not 'after a sort, divided into parishes', so that to speak of Christ anywhere was an encroachment upon localized religion. All the same, Wesley had been made touchy by being told that 'Our brethren in Fetter-Lane being in great confusion for want of my presence and advice.' Guilt. Our three parishes here may indeed be part of 'all the world' yet their parochiality remains firmly fixed within their boundaries. Indeed, it requires a self-conscious degree of charity to allow any loss of boundary in the average united benefice, the grouping of villages being seen as unnatural and a recent bit of diocesan fiddle-faddle. Who in their right mind would say that Wormingford, Mount Bures and Little Horkesley were historically 'united'? That is the last thing they were. Of course, 'we are all one in Him,' but that is different.

I catch up on the parish news. From each village its own news. Just as I thought, it is sensational. It has to be. A parochial prerogative is that something must happen the minute one turns one's back, and it has. I show the requisite amazement. A nave ceiling has been painted cobalt, a cake-stall has been a goldmine, the hymns I had chosen for 'Songs of Praise' had been lopped, 'Otherwise we'd be singing them still', and the churchwardens had been heard muttering, 'He won't like it; he says the words are poems.' But he understands – is he not parochial? What does astonish me is the garden. Having left it trim and in bud, I come back to find it modelling for Monet and the cat high on pollen. My new rose 'John Clare' is in full bloom, Clare the ultimate parish voice of England, the poet who was able to make village limitations illimitable. It was he who wrote that moving hymn 'The Stranger' in which Christ becomes the outcast villager who is forced to leave his own home boundaries. John Clare was both the prisoner and the free spirit of the parochialism, both narrowly confined and liberated. A line from his sad hymn: 'The blind met daylight in His eye.'

Deanery Evensong

'Summer afternoon – summer afternoon; to me those have always been the two most beautiful words in the English language,' confesses an Edith Wharton character. After lunch I check their verity in the garden. A skylark sings half a mile up and there is the tower of Stoke-by-Nayland making its usual Impressionist blue smudge in the distance. In our churchyard a small army of Sunday walkers have halted at John Nash's grave. Someone is speaking and pointing. It is warm, late afternoon. On to Little Horkesley where a sizeable army of choirs from miles around are mustering for the yearly Deanery Evensong, a tremendous event, as no one needs telling, and this year swollen by Coggeshall. These Coggeshallians are princely in red and can sing. It is a known fact. They loll against our best tombs as more sparkling hot cars bump their way into Mr Eddis's meadow, and as the bells crash forth. I, as I habitually do, pause inside the church to pay my respects to three vast oaken de Horkesleys who have lain side by side since 1250, only to discover that their fearsome brows have been bound with daisy-chains. I once dreamed that they were breathing as I passed, their wooden breasts moving in deep sleep. Strange clergymen arrive for, make no bones about it, six miles from us it is all another country, deanery or no deanery. All the doors are wide and the congregation sits in cross-currents. The first hymn can hardly be described as a processional as the choir fills the building from chancel to porch, rather as on Trinity Sunday the Lord's train in Isaiah's vision filled the temple. And so it is, and in spite of its being evensong, delectable summer afternoon.

An old fellow near me, a Coggeshallian without a doubt, sings the entire service, hymns, psalm, liturgy, anthem and all sans book. Every verse, every word. I am awed. Gordon heard someone behind him murmur to his wife, 'Back to the usual next week.' Of course. It cannot be always summer afternoon, summer afternoon, with young Bishop Heber and with Bishop Rorison's 'Light of Lights', and daisy-chains round medieval foreheads, and St Mark's great cry, and the Spirit like a dove descending, even if it should be, ideally speaking.

I take my life into my hands as the Deanery surges out by telling the farmers that the coldest spring in memory will only have delayed the harvest, not threatened it. Farmers like a bit of gloom, so they look at me reproachfully. Mad cows, mad poets. 'When did we last have rain? Tell me that.' They hoist themselves into their Range Rovers like the misjudged. The Coggeshallians, too, fold their robes and steal away. It is still summer afternoon at midnight.

Trinity One: St Barnabas

And so, as John Meade Falkner (the onlie begetter of Betjeman?) says,

> We have done with dogma and divinity
>   Easter and Whitsun past,
> The long, long Sundays after Trinity
>   Are with us at last;
> The passionless Sundays after Trinity
>   Neither feast-day nor fast.

A beguiling poem by a curate's son who became a Victorian arms dealer before finding salvation in literature. However, these long, long Sundays begin far from passionlessly. The Apostle, stranded on Patmos, hears a voice like a trumpet 'talking with me' and saying, 'Come hither . . .' I am frequently tempted to say 'Come hither' to those spokesmen who continue to confine human history to the Christian era, and to take them to a severe bend in the river where this year's crops take root in fields which seem to grow flints. For those who lived here the Incarnation was thousands of years hence. An apologist for the new Catechism from Rome excuses its tone by declaring, as usual, that the Church has to 'think in centuries'. Only centuries? And when a thousand ages in God's sight are like an evening gone? On my way to the flint fields, I pause a moment to smell the honeysuckles which have completely encaged two Georgian tombs. Faint sunshine plays once more on the Roman quoins which square-up the tower. In the light of my destination, they are close to becoming the latest thing. In the fancifulness which plays around with hard facts and breeds vision, they could have been baked when Domitian sentenced John to a spell in the salt-mines. In actuality, as 'man-made stone', they would have presented a dazzling human achievement to the community, already long lost in time, who dwelt in the elbow of the river, splashing, shouting in its shallows. I found a kind of smoothing tool which fitted my palm perfectly. It was lying among a million other stones but could not hide itself. A warm hand had shaped it. I sat on the bank in the unique silence of deserted habitations, and this one dated only from later prehistory. Trinity Sundays slow us down, maybe, but they also beckon to what is immeasurable with their 'Come hither'. For me, archaeology is one way of going forward.

Flower Festival Again

Sturdy women are out hammering posters all along the main roads leading to the village like Lorelei to lure the passing motorist. Gillian and her reaper band are in my garden cutting car-loads of foliage and dragging luscious hanks of marsh marigold from my horse-pond. The vicar and I sit at the dining-table surrounded by hymn-books because the Flower Festival must have *Songs of Praise*. This year it is our intention to autocratically impose our choice on the congregation because on the occasions when it did the choosing the result was, well, limited. Michael and I both love hymns and this year we shall 'box and cox' our way through this sacred sing-song. We soon discover that a mutual favourite, 'Ye servants of God', is in neither the *English Hymnal* nor *Hymns for Today*, so shame on their editors. It shall be run off on the school photocopier and, what is more, we shall process in with it. The 'great congregation' – we hope – His triumph shall sing to a heartening tune from the *Paderborn Gesangbuch*. We shall also include John Clare's hymn 'The Stranger' in which the isolation of Christ is underlyingly informed by the isolation of the poet himself. We sang it when Ted Hughes unveiled Clare's memorial in Westminster Abbey and he and I both thought how astonished that unrivalled, simple poet of the fields would have been to know that his name would share a space with Matthew Arnold's. Time sorts us all out. The true and excellent remain.

Our bitter spring has given way to benign winds and rains. The fruit blossom has been prodigious but all the other flowers have been held back a fortnight or more. The arrangers discover buds where they hoped to find blooms, and become frantic. They can be caught staring at my still-closed and waiting heads as though wondering if a couple of days in the nave might encourage them to come out. I have in the past notoriously suggested cow parsley and was instantly ruled out as an adviser. Say what you like, it does go with Gothic. However, as all males know, their business at flower festivals is to fetch and carry, and not air their daft ideas. I fill a huge pot with cow parsley and bluebells and place it defiantly on a ledge in what used to be the farm kitchen, and Max lies under it until his black fur is starry with pollen – better this than sitting high up in trees terrifying nesting birds. How are they to know that he hates feathers? He has a shocking reputation as a tree-cat and it is not uncommon for visitors to look skywards when they hope to meet him. Michael, the vicar, and his wife Shirley have four cats, or maybe five. Cats come on holiday to our vicarage. 'How would you like that, Max?' An aghast look.

St Alban

We picnic between services at Sawyer's under enamelled skies. This ancient farm has for me all the ramified interests and connections which come from a lifetime's friendships within a small group. It is where an old friend's uncles, Geoffrey and Martin Shaw, worked on their hymns and carols during the twenties. It is also a few yards from where the youthful Thomas Gainsborough sat to paint his 'Cornard Wood'. A dizzy marker, the BBC's television mast for our area, gives the exact positioning of Sawyer's when I look for it across the valley. Today it all bathes in the Trinity warmth and I see that the wheat has gone 'blue' – that intermittent turquoise which

June brings out between the greening and the bronzing. The panoramic fields are empty of humanity, of course. I suppose we have some 800 souls in our three parishes and that, at a guess, there cannot be more than forty of them who work the land. At this time of the year not so very long ago the countryside would have been swarming with piece-workers, pickers, itinerants, all those wandering flocks of seasonal toilers who picked their way across summer England. Everywhere one went there would be folk 'tiffling' about with this or that – i.e. doing lots of important little jobs without *over*doing it by way of energy. But now not a sound of labour or of idleness. Just the whispering corn being self-sufficient, and all the villagers away in towns.

Except for myself, of course. But it is a well-known fact that writers, artists and the like have a fine old time of it, lolling about, reading books and such like, and being paid for it. The man who came to mend something had been in Spain for a week. 'But I expect for you, sir, it is all holiday.' I had to agree.

I am rereading Thomas Traherne and 'up to here' in his ecstatic landscape. This burst of summer is reproducing it in the village. I like the poet's occasionally scalding tone. We are not to be 'Blind, and dead and Dull, and foolish ... and Accustomed unto narrow things'. Wherever we may be we must 'Restore thine image, recall our minds'. In other words God needs not only to see his face but some of his intelligence reflected in us.

Trinity Two

To Westminster Abbey for a nice rest after the demands of a rustic united benefice. Bull-daisies all the way. Tea with the Maynes and the Tomlinsons, Charles half-lost in what he is going to say when we reach Poets' Corner which is going to be extended in an original manner. More anon. The Dean rescues confirmation-class booklets from the chairs and Elizabeth I glares down. Charles and I discover a mutual admiration for Willa Cather's marvellous novel *Death Comes for the Archbishop*, and for R. S. Thomas. Then a drifting procession to evensong through the holiday-makers with their tilted faces. The introit is sung off-stage, as it were, distant, unseen, ravishing. An appalling first lesson from Joshua about a massacre of the people of Ai. It is Rwanda long ago, and God-commanded, which I do not believe.

Then to the south transept to write the names Robert Herrick and Alexander Pope on coloured glass to inaugurate an extension of Poets' Corner. Alison and I sit in the front row with our feet on Dylan Thomas, and Charles Tomlinson gives the address. Every inch of floor and wall space is memorialized and, in the untidy way of writers, nobody keeps to his age. Olympian dust is disorderly and Herrick's and Pope's, for some unexplained reason, have taken centuries to float here. Tim Pigott-Smith reads from *Hesperides* and *The Dunciad*, and a veil falls to reveal the new glassy chapter to a national book of honour which began to be written in this transept when a young undergraduate took it on himself to rehouse Chaucer's bones in the present fine tomb. The coming into view and the going out of consideration of poets is evident here. It happened to poor Herrick in his lifetime, he the goldsmith's golden son and forgotten survivor of the Golden Age who was turned out

of his Devon rectory to arrive back in the London he so missed with a poetry that had gone out of fashion. None of that Christian–Faerie–Classical–Bruegelish stuff for a Commonwealth. Fluorescent Robert, with his verses filled with English summer scent, and his girls, and his drink, and his meadowy opulence. From his shimmering window-plate he can wink across to his old hero Ben Jonson. The choirboys arrive to sing Herrick's 'Sweet spirit, comfort me!' Pope's brilliant lozenge is inscribed, 'Heav'n is won by violence of song'. Who will join them up there? A great many. Tim rides back to Regent's Park on his motor bike, where he is producing *Hamlet* and where they are digging Ophelia's grave.

Trinity Three: George Herbert

Gordon and I have driven over the high ground to present a George Herbert Evensong at White Colne – 'White' after a *Dimidius Blanctus* from the Middle Ages. Heat lies in the corn, turning its stalks blue. They have rough-cut the little churchyard for the occasion and modest stones can be read. There is a tradition here of simplicity. 'Earls Colne may have its Earls, White Colne nothing at all' and the Bemerton which Herbert found rushes to mind. A lot of folk, including many old women, descendants of Anna whose widowhood becomes a kind of dedication in rural temples. Two small worried children in the choir – 'Have you lost something?' – 'Yes, our parents.' What can you expect of parents; they will wander all over the place. There must be grandparents here who are the last of the workers from the 'horse' farming. So many summer frocks, so many rose-white heads.

We sing the Herbert hymns with their compressed metaphysics and I read him from the pulpit without analysis, 'Giddinesse', 'Artillerie', 'The Flower', 'Love' and other poems, then talk about his own compressed enchantment with Christ. No time to be expansive when one has to cram all one's experience of the companionship of the Lord in a ministry of just under three years. An unspoken recognition of various lines in the poems flashes across my brain as their wholeness floods the pretty nave, and I have to resist being schoolteacherly. 'I, who had heard of musick in the spheres, and not of speech in stars', for example. How had Herbert heard that the planets sing? From Kepler, a contemporary enchanter, of course. But what I chiefly think about is a long wander in Wiltshire a decade ago and sitting in Dauntsey parish church, where deacon George said his office and played his lute, and kneeling in Bemerton where the ploughmen knelt, having tied up their horses to the hedge. What did they make of him, this lanky, black-haired Welsh gentleman coughing his heart out, riding high on Sarum, striding through the water-meadows once a week to sing in Salisbury Cathedral, ringing his own bell, and in such a clean cassock? So what is the old poet telling us? That our Christ has to be the fellow-traveller of the Emmaus road. Afterwards, in the porch, there are hugs and recognitions. We all go back a long way.

St John the Baptist

True summer with every old rose in its profusion. I sprawl by a gooseberry bush reading the Penguin *St Anselm*. What long prayers, what openness, what alarming intimacies. I am also reading in my unfaithful way Sylvia Townsend Warner's *The Corner That Held Them*, her witty novel about some irritable medieval women founding a nunnery in the Fens. I should be weeding, but it is true summer at last and between Anselm's naked petitions and the squabbling at Oby I fall into lassitude. True summer is as much sounds as scents. There is an over-layering of soft noises, of a west wind covering a clapping of poplar leaves, of the little waterfall sounds tumbling across the drone of the haymaker. The about-to-flower *Hypericum perforatum* reminds me that the herald of Christ is about to arrive, a summer child who 'was wonderfully born', and who will be 'a burning and shining light'. Just like his emblematic plant, in fact. There is so much of it here that I have had to tie it against a bay-tree in order to get to the house. Unseen thrushes crash around in the bay-tree, adding to the sound upon sound. A plane joins in for a few bars and leaves its own silence. I glory in my sloth and thank God that I am not with those Prioresses (they all had a turn) at Oby in the fourteenth century, and who were very noisy ladies.

I find Anselm's prayer to the divine herald and am taken aback by its vehemence:

> St John:
> you are that John who baptized God
> . . . you knew God before you knew the world
> . . . to you, sir, who are so great . . .
> comes a guilty, creeping thing,
> a wretched little man.

One of our village churches is dedicated to the Baptist and some Tractarian has placed a lean statue of him near the altar. A trickle of a brook flows in the meadow below with hardly enough water for his vast Jordan acts. At matins I will speak about this summer birthday, the ageing mother, the dumbstruck father, the role of forerunner. And with a bit of luck the weather will hold out and the sun and the *Hypericum* will exchange glances, and we guilty, creeping things will hang up the bell-ropes, sign the register, hark to some of each other's troubles and call it a Sunday. It is the season of strangers, of quiet ramblers and holiday-makers in discreet attendance in the back pews. 'Somebody can sing!' we say appreciatively.

Grass

The great meadow is being mowed. Keith and Bernard clatter up and down its plunging acres on a machine which throws out burnt brown rectangular hay biscuits.

> A voice says, 'Cry!'
> 'What shall I cry?'
> 'All flesh is grass.'

A tolerable image of transience. The washing bleaches on the lawn, the gooseberries are being gathered with the blackbirds looking on, thousands of old roses perfume the slight wind. Dark William Lob, delicate Celestine, rich Charles de Mille, susceptible Leda, modest John Clare, the latest to arrive in the garden. We have staggered home from yet one more flower

festival at Mount Bures. Few in this high village have much notion of 'arrangement' in today's semi-professional terms and so we see something absolutely different, and flawless of its kind. Vicki read from the Song of Songs and John from the Lord's attack on materialism in Luke 12. Whilst Diana preached on a horticultural philosophy of life. Outside, the 'Mount', shaggy with brambles, cast long shadows over the graves of the congregation before the present one. If its flesh is indeed grass, then it is the best silky, tidy grass. We listen to the click-clack and whistle of the Sudbury train as it reaches our crossing but nobody glances at his watch. Nobody says, as they once did, 'What do you make it? I make it half a minute late.'

I have finished a book. A novel. And I do not feel as I am supposed to feel, that I have made and lost, or done with, a child. Rather I feel as some people do when the guests have gone, released. I think of all the things I shall do with no book to cry 'Write me!' as soon as I get up. I might read all the books which have been waiting for me to read this last year. Although I am not likely to be as deplorable as the late Jean Rhys and sit on the floor drinking gin at breakfast and browsing in old tales, smoking like a trooper and not giving a damn. But I might lie under the poplars to hear their summery clapping, one of the loveliest sounds in the world, and an immortal one I am sure. And I shall certainly consider the grasses as well as the lilies. If our flesh is to transmigrate, where better than to the rich greening of the world?

Haymaking

Up at six these warm, blowy mornings, the prisoners to release. These are Charles's or Elspeth's or Harold's bees which have become trapped overnight in the double-glazing, plus a few moths and butterflies. The post arrives and is enough to break one's heart. A huge two-feet-square of a letter from British Telecom to say, 'We are cutting 10 per cent off your business calls' and a much re-used envelope from an old friend which reads 'Save the Trees'. Also a card from Richard Mabey whose whole life is given to environmental teaching, plus a big manila packet from a cathedral containing two lines on the date of a committee meeting. Taste, waste and ignorance make their customary bow between the tea and the toast. There is also a lovely fat book from the poet–philosopher William Anderson.

They are making hay at Maltings Farm, at the Grange and at the Hall. 'The hay appeareth, and the tender grass showeth itself, as the haymaker drones up and down across the pastures. Green has bleached to near-white and the machine leaves the meadows looking like combed blond hair. It is the feast of grass, the festival of the Gramineae, that least individually recognized of plants. The many species tumble into polleny ranks whilst the blades cut on. To make hay is to make merry and also to make metaphors for our own impermanence. In scripture the rich and wasteful have their noses rubbed in it, so to speak. For hay is splendour laid low. We have proper hay-meadows and set-aside. The latter is a constant disappointment where I am concerned, for I always hope that it would produce a rare flower or two. But at Sawyers and below Tiger Hill the succulent hay-meadows of the past have been encouraged to return, and the machines rumble into an intoxication of grasses, clovers and bull-daisies. When we were children certain flowers had 'to go with something' and bull-daisies had to go with quaking-grass. It was a law. These still grow side by side in Boulge churchyard and close to the roses from Omar Khayyám's tomb which enclose the grave of Edward FitzGerald. Years ago I had to sit in FitzGerald's cottage at haymaking time to dole out the prizes for the local flower show, nearly every one of which went to two fearsomely competitive farmworkers. Where the poet was concerned, all flesh was less grass than rose-petals. He has a line from the *Jubilate* on his tomb – 'It is He that hath made us, and not we ourselves,' by which his family could have intended, 'Don't blame him for being so odd.'

Bliss – to sprawl on one's stomach in a haymeadow and give names to the grass family, the sweet-grasses, the fescues, the ryes.

Flora's Wedding

Summertime and the livin' is easy. Or would be if half rural England was not up to its signboards in organizing an Event. Maybe one day at a village funeral the ultimate accolade will be awarded: 'He never arranged an event.' The local paper is one vast importuning of events, so lie low. And what of the perils of overlap? Flora's wedding overlaps the school fête, or vice versa. Had it just been a matter of traffic in the narrow lane, a clash between bellringing and fête music, a way out might have been found. But what can anyone do but clear the path for a walking bridal procession headed by a fiddler. The bridal way home is via the meadows, now soaking after no more than a spit of rain, thus wet feet beneath the majestic green dress and thrown-back old veil. The tall bridegroom strides forth and the lively violinist draws wondering looks from the cows. What cows can make of human behaviour the dear Lord only knows.

I was about to set off to Flora's wedding when the head-teacher telephones to ask will I judge the children's fancy-dress? When I tell her that I shall be giving the address at that very moment I sense the fleeting possibility in her (teachers must be possiblists, else where would education be?) that, no matter, I might still be able to make a dash from church to school during the signing of the register, declare First Prize and return without anyone being the wiser. Has not Michael the vicar, after all, managed to open the fête and to get back in time to welcome Flora at the church door? But I point out that he runs in the London Marathon. What outdoes the fancy-dress from over the road is the fancy-dress in the nave. Can this really be my old friend Charles – this magnificent person straight out of Trollope? He is the bride's father. Can this be her mother with big red roses from my garden swaying on her hat? And surely that young man with the fiery beard and the genuine 1880s frock coat must hurry from here to preach on Sin in Spurgeon's Tabernacle? The bride's brothers, equally trans-formed by tailoring, exercise a Christian restraint which I had not seen in them before when she promises to obey, and do not exchange grins. Ruth's exquisite tribute to her mother-in-law is read. I then reveal that the very first marriage in our Worm-ingford register was between William Lufte and Margaret Army-dyl on 'Saint Peters Dai in the first year of the Rayne of our Soverayne Lady Queen Eliz'th', and that this is St Peter's Day 1996 and there are Philip and Flora kneeling in all their youthful stateliness beneath the very same arch and making the very same vows. The literary Irish relations being present, I read from Edmund Spenser's *Epithalamion*, the poet's own marriage poem. Robust stuff. Laughter. Then faint cries from the school fête. Then fiddle music. 'Where shall I stand?' asks the violinist.

Trinity Four: St Peter

A fenland interval as I write to John Seaman, Vicar of Parson Drove with Murrow and Guyhirn. It is about an address I gave on Thomas Traherne in the Puritan Chapel at Guyhirn, a scrubbed, stark little building near Wisbech so unclouded by time that one can almost smell the snowy linen of the Huguenot saints, and where the seats are purposely set too close for kneeling or any nonsense of that sort. Plain windows stare out at Lincolnshire and Cambridgeshire. There is no light except daylight, and, as my old friend Edward Storey the poet remarked, it is odd to call it a chapel of ease. I told Mr Seaman's congregation which comes to pray here annually, about Traherne, who was twenty-three when it was built, and who is a master of the Affirmative way. Traherne seduces for God. Beware his *Centuries* if you cannot admit to the gloriousness of being alive. I read the matchless passage beginning 'The Corn was Orient and Immortal Wheat, which never should be reaped, nor was ever sown. I thought it stood from Everlasting to Everlasting,' a language so extravagant that I thought I would soon be called to order by a shocked Walloon fen-drainer. 'What rule do you think I walk by?' Traherne asked his friend Mrs Hopton. 'By the study of God's goodness in the most obvious and common things, sir, light, Heaven, Earth, water, the Sun, trees, men, women, cities, temples . . .' I read his Tyburn-theatre view of Calvary, which is heartbreaking, a prose version of the glass in King's College Chapel a few miles off, which ends shockingly with 'Can this be an Entertainment!' (*Century* One, para. 89).

Patronals

My sister, back in Suffolk after many years in Sydney, says that we must go to Bury St Edmunds to call on old friends. These include Mary Tudor, Queen of France, tucked away in the corner of St Mary's church, the carpet-bedding in the Abbey Gardens, the glass case in the museum containing the relics of the Red Barn murder – 'Polstead cherries! Polstead cherries!' they used to shout in the market-place when we were children, 'Red as Maria Martin's blood!' – the River Lark sulkily winding under the Abbot's bridge, and the theatre where *Charley's Aunt* first raised the roof. *En route*, we drove past the high ground where our ancestors ploughed and where all their remote lives they enjoyed a huge view. How puzzled they would have been that we were in Bury 'on a Monday'. You only went to town on a market-day. We stood on the lawn which was the chapter-house, so called because it was where a chapter from St Benedict's Rule was read each morning. Like appallingly bad teeth, the rubble stumps of the Abbey aisles stood all around us, all that remains of one of Christendom's mightiest buildings. The air was filled with the scent of *Philadelphus* and old roses, and with the cries of little boys balancing on ruins.

Back home it is patronal time, with Peter on the heels of John the Baptist. As is well known, attending and helping-out another church's patronal festival is a major act of Christian charity. It also allows for leisurely observation of what they get up to down the lane. Since each of our parishes is inimitable and could not be like its neighbour if it tried, the faint anxiety which attaches to our patronal efforts is hard to understand. But there it is, as an old man always ends up, there it is. The immutable, I suppose he means. That which has to be put up with.

It has been a week of rites of passage, with young people coming to enquire about being baptized, then confirmed, then receiving the sacraments, then getting married. All on one day? 'If you like.' More than ever, it seems to me, the Church must *educate*. Must disengage from recent pap and match the high intelligence of those who seek for God.

At Lelant

A once-visited place can be among the least faded pages of one's autobiography. When I was twenty my mother and I walked from Newlyn to St Ives, having been assured on the telephone that the sun was shining there. Newlyn, only eight miles away, was cold and thick with sea-fog. So we walked out of it, passing through Lelant and emerging, as they promised, into the unique light of St Ives Bay. I can still feel the exultation, the feeling of accomplishment. The higgledy-piggledy little town, custom-built for herring fishermen lay before us, and every view filled a well-known canvas. Lelant that day was no more than a name along the road, but now, half a lifetime later, is the destination. Someone on the radio had been saying that the proper archaeologist not only notes every disturbance of the soil before he reaches the occupant of a grave but, with luck, will be able to note the footprints of the man who dug it.

It is late evening when we arrive in Lelant and all the footprints of the day are waiting to be obliterated by the tide. But time has not put out the two forms of illumination which caught my eye when I last passed this way, the intermittent beam from Virginia Woolf's lighthouse, and the unblinking sparks of the glow-worms along the sandy path. These are lady glow-worms telling their blacked-out mates where they are. All along the heathy edge, this shameless golden stare. And to the right, Hayle glittering like Eldorado, and to the left, just seeable on its eminence, a tiny chapel built for St Nicholas against which I sat in my youth, bewitched by Cornwall. This visit I explore St Uny's church in Lelant, to discover that it would all have filled up with sand had it not been for a golfing parson who taught his parishioners how to turn dunes into links, a miracle which would have delighted Betjeman. St Uny's churchyard is what the botanists call 'flower rich' – that kind of turf which, alas, can only be found in specialist areas at home. But here it is the norm. Such clovers and orchises, such poppies, scabious and bedstraw dense on the ground. And popping up like jack-in-the-boxes all around, jolly golfers whose voices carry across the tombs.

At meals there is the luxury of listening to parish matters one doesn't know the first thing about, human failings, deanery business, liturgical practices, this kind of thing. Thank heavens I remembered to give Mrs Cardy the hymn-list before going to Lelant. A colleague at the school governors' meeting said, 'You're going *away*?' Yes, far away to where I used to be, and am thus able to claim a foothold. To where all those sainted Cornish clergymen had to shout the Gospel against howling winds and wailing gulls.

St Swithun

Mr Chaplin clangs two medieval bells. *Sancte Necolae Ora Pro Nobis* takes turns with *Sit Nomen Domini Benedictum*, a courtesy observed since 1460. It is all the bell-music there has ever been at Mount Bures. Mr Chaplin is eighty-five and without a white hair, and he has succeeded Jim who departed at eighty, which is no age at all. I wait unseen in the vestry until the ancient noise ceases and then, allowing a minute for Mr Chaplin to find his pew, descend steeply into the cool church. It smells of baked churchyard and has trapped within it some of the blue of the harebells which, in July, form a kind of cloudless sky at foot level. The heatwave devours the hilltop even at this hour of the morning and we can hear the drone of a barley-cutter. There are a dozen of us to be moved by scripture in this particular sundry place, and moved we are because Andrew has to read the Song of Deborah and Barak, a terrible ballad all about a woman tricking a hunted captain into what he believes is a safe haven and then driving a tent-peg through his temple as he sleeps, nailing his head to her floor. Andrew does not stumble at this but approaches names such as 'Issachar' and 'Naphtali' warily. Jim used to plough through such verbal obstructions head-on, sending syllables flying in all directions. Surely the elderly women in their summery frocks are going to faint when Jael picks up 'the workman's hammer', but no. Andrew's ghastly words float over them because they have been seized by reverie and have been struck senseless by sunshine. Liturgy is playing its pranks in their devout heads and spinning holy day-dreams around them. I try to take my mind off the tent-peg by concentrating on the kaleidoscopic colours which the east window casts upon a wall-tablet to children who perished during some Georgian epidemic. I hear Andrew conclude: 'And the land had rest forty years.' So maybe Deborah had something to sing about.

During the intercessions I read George Appleton's fine prayer for 'the casualties of history'. I can hear the UN troops digging-in above Sarajevo as I say it and human beings being turned out into meadows, and the everlasting racket of war. 'O God, my mind and spirit fail in the thought of all the casualties of history ... If thou art not a God of mercy, redemption and love, my pain is incurable. But I am comforted in the thought that the creature cannot rise higher than his Creator . . .' The formularies of worship and of violence, how we hold to them. 'And the land had rest forty years' – what is that? We are not displeased to find it hotter than ever outside. Those who dwell in an equitable climate like its deviations to be extreme.

Trinity Five

A midsummer's night and the village all asleep. We are early birds. Commuters must drive off to the station from five a.m., farmworkers (few of these) must bump down the tracks an hour or two later, children must catch school buses at eight. Here and there a blue flicker through thin curtains betrays the late film. Standing at a high window, I am wooed by owls, tawny ones by the sound of their sumptuously deep, Melba-like *hoos*. One is close to the house and preaching desolation. The haunting cry reminds me of Isaiah's description of the fall of Edom. Change the architecture and it might well be a description of the long-abandoned farm-buildings site which lies just below me. 'And thorns shall come up in palaces, nettles and brambles in the fortress ... and it shall be ... a court for owls.' But blackberries from last year's brambles fill the deep-freeze and bricks from the footings of tumbled pigsties will, this autumn, make fine paths. The nearest owl will have none of this; desolation it must be. His wild cry is answered far away with matching comfortlessness by an owl sailing through purple clouds to Bures. A small boy staring upwards: 'Birds don't know it's Friday.' Well, thank goodness for that. These midnight owls certainly would not consider themselves to be lost in wastes and fit company for poor Job. They are mousing on the wing.

It is a night for a discreet wander – one must never forget the scandal caused by the Wordsworths and Coleridge at Nether Stowey by their nocturnal ramblings. That they were composing *Lyrical Ballads* was no excuse. I pray that Penny's dog is under lock and key. Wild roses festoon every hedge and cats emerge from ditches with golden glances at this late person. It is sultry and every window is wide. The church tower is a charcoal

stump, just as it was during the summer nights which followed the Conquest. The clock face gives me its old-fashioned look. Gravestones are legible and there are dense scents. Young rabbits are dining off a wreath and other unidentifiable creatures rustle and fidget. Everywhere, it is all so perfectly interesting that one might never go to bed.

On the bridge which links Essex to Suffolk I lean over to observe the pull of the currents and the tiny shoals of perch and dench darting through the reed-mace. A sound from our neighbour church at Little Horkesley floats on the water. Bell-tongues and owls-songs join.

Parish Records

'History is now and England,' stated Eliot. An event this Whitsun week brought to mind my move to a Suffolk farmhouse and the prompt arrival of an ancient man with sky-blue eyes to 'give you a hand with the grass', i.e. to find out who I was. Very wise. Rumour having put it about that I wrote books, he was mildly awed. Then, spotting the typewriter, it was, 'Aha!' Any fool could write books with a machine. He himself had never written a word in his life, nor read one. What is more, they – he meant a succession of scribbling vicars – had failed to put him down. What did I think of that? I congratulated him. Later, he would take me to a barn to show me his fourteen-year-old handprint in the plaster and declare triumphantly, 'That's all!' He meant evidence of his existence. I was taught some wonderful local history by this unlettered neighbour.

A fat envelope arrives from the *Victoria County History of Essex*, begun in 1903 and still in progress – one should not rush these things – and it contains queries which I as the appointed recorder for Wormingford must answer. Never before have I seen such a complete and scholarly account of our parish, and I read it avidly, the manors and farms tumbling from hand to hand through the centuries, the clear dating of the Methodists' tin chapel, the tale of our spire, the year that they took down Bowden's farmhouse and shipped it to New England. The time when the farmers prevented the vicar from opening a school because literacy would make the labourers hard to handle. Extraordinary figures galloped through our lanes early on, knights from Poitou, Queen Eleanor, a Lord Plaiz, scores of Waldegraves, and properties were in constant transition via death or the market. My queries-to-be-answered are less romantic. The dates of the council houses, when did we go on the mains? etc. I at once telephone Ken who has lived in the same house since 1924 and who is both by birth and aptitude our true village recorder, and we have an extended learned chat which begins with drains and ends with cricket. I tell him about the *Victoria County History*, volume ten now actually in progress, and he tells me that we should have all our Wormingford books and photos put into a nice locked glass case in the Village Hall, to which I answer Amen.

I sleep with all the windows wide and the timeless sounds of the valley can be heard, fox-cries, owl-cries, the very late and the very early birds, the splashing of the stream and of course the thudding of hooves. It is only Lord Plaiz or Queen Eleanor or a Waldegrave passing by. It is actually Jean's mare stamping her restlessness into the pasture.

Trinity Six

'Oo go to Jericho' mother would say when we exasperated her, meaning, 'Get out of my sight!' We fled. 'And be back by teatime!' We have all been down to Jericho these last few days – it is down to Jericho and up to Jerusalem – following Yasser Arafat to his new old capital. It was there before Abraham, a city founded around a well from which the Lord would have quenched his thirst. It flickers on the screen, dun, noisy, hot, one of the first towns on earth. But I see its parched setting to be exactly the same colour as English barley fields in mid-July. These are at their rustling perfection and near to being cut. As in Ruth's time it is barley first, then wheat. Ruth gleaned barley-stalks – and young Boaz the farmer. As children on long country walks to grandmother's house we found barley sympathetic. It tickled our bare legs, not scratched them white as did the corn. Its dusty sibilance was the sound of a whispering sea and its hue just before the reaper went in, a lion's-mane tan.

Except for the annual theatre of yellow rape, blue flax and mauve borage – 'Why are you growing borage, Hugh?' 'For Pimm's Number One' – the village at this moment sits on a baking palette containing every shade of brown. Considering the brownness of Palestine, one marvels that it is never mentioned in scripture. Just brown cows in Genesis. Greenness is what these sacred writings emphasize. Our pastures are a cool emerald among the tawny crops whose sunny browns shade into surrounding parishes and make a good match with those of Jericho. Such ripeness has its poignant side; what is ripe must fall, must be gathered, must go.

Distant traffic roars up and down to 'themes', it being impossible nowadays it seems to have a country outing which is not thematic. The air is sultry and the verges are stuck with little notices begging the traveller to make his way to traction-engine parks, farm-walks, flower-filled churches, fêtes, teas, open gardens, rallies, Tudor banquets, pick-your-own fruits. Anywhere except, if he is like me, to where he would like to go. Which is just on. Past all such diversions and into the pleasantly listless distances of July, with the rose-bay willow-herb filling dry ditches and the loud bird-music of summer. Rural leisure has reached such a pitch that one may soon have to wear a badge – IDNWTBE – I do not wish to be entertained. I am in a brown study.

The Dozers and the Dancers

'Why should I let the toad *work*/Squat on my life?' asked Larkin famously. I have never yet lived anywhere in the country where a particular local family does not concur to the letter, and customarily over several generations. We toilers regard it with a mixture of censure and envy. That house where the postman apologizes when he disturbs its rest at ten a.m. That house in which the generations come and go, and nothing whatever is done. Delightful children rush around before, at about eighteen, they happily slow down to their drone-inheritance. Natural workers occasionally intermarry with these strict non-workers and are permitted to continue to rush about on the condition that they do not bring their busy-ness home, or carp about sloth. 'Good morning,' I say (although it is usually afternoon when I pass) to the amiable shapes sunning themselves in gardens where nothing too exhausting is ever done. Sweet smiles and a kindly wave of the hand. Once, with real concern, 'Have you walked all the way?' Their dog flops over at the very thought of it. We agree that there is not a breath of air, that we could do with a good rain, and similar vacuities.

The village bakes and I can hear the barley rustling, the monotonous voice of the chiff-chaff and other minor noises. I feel the languor of July doing its best to hold me up. The poetry of inertia arrives in listless fragments, everything from Addison's 'When in the sultry glebe I faint', to my favourite, 'We have done with dogma and divinity'.

I have to step gingerly where five young men are furiously tarring the lane. The heat is terrific and the tar smells nice. A sultry glebe would be a treat in comparison but these workers patch and mend with energy, dancing about between their sticky islands whilst fore and aft the irritable traffic builds up. The platitude here is, 'No sooner do we get a bit of warm weather than they have the road up.' Torpor is called for but the tar-men spray and dance, and the road is far from 'up' – it is liquid. I share something with these tarrers because I too tend to dance about, no matter how sultry the glebe. Tennyson's lotus-eaters 'Came unto a land in which it seemed always afternoon.' I must go on a course on lotus-eating. The cat pants in the shade. The toad work would receive short shrift if it settled on him.

The Barley Harvest

L ate July, the time of tall flowers, convolvulus tangles, strong southerlies and first harvests. People say, 'They are cutting at Langham' – or wherever. Combines, whose active life is on a par with that of the dragonfly, are being lured from their huge sheds. They put me in mind of May-days in Padstow when the ''Oss' would be tempted from its hiding-place to sway and dance through the ecstatic town. The 'Oss's coming to life, albeit for just a day, brings tears to Cornish eyes. Where the combine is concerned, it would be its failure to start or cut which would make the farmer weep. It groans its way into the barley leaving not so much as an ear for Ruth, whilst Boaz sways aloft. Translating such harvests into festivals is no easy task. Some unmasticated barley stalks are rescued for decorating the church. Strolling through the undoubtedly bounteous fields, the parched cereal scratches my legs and hands as it did when

I was a boy, and there is the same revelling in the dip and sway of ripened landscape as the wind passes over it. At night I can hear the heart-stoppingly wild cries of foxes. I rescue a bat from Max, who can't think what to do with it, having caught it, and is bewildered by its very existence. I place the bat on a ledge of the tumbledown granary, where it palpitates like a scrap of velvet caught in a draught. I can see what the cat is thinking – 'More inedible even than a shrew'.

A young couple arrives. Can they be baptized, confirmed

and wed? Next year will do. Far from youthful friends with the mark of sickness and hospitals visible, talk bravely under the limes. An ancient lady tells me that she has *two* bottles of whisky in her cupboard. I reel back in horror. 'They were from my wedding, dear [at least sixty years ago]. But I've never tasted Drink, dear. No never.' She says that she doesn't know what she would do 'without my God'. I know nothing of her past, only her present, which has a kind of rough radiance. I find myself thinking of her as I give the annual John Clare Lecture at Helpston, and of the poet's liking to work beside motherly women as they weeded the crops because he could listen to their stories. It was Clare who identified himself with the vagrant Christ, a fugitive Lord who, although 'the blind met daylight in his eye', encountered inhospitality. In the lecture I call Clare the July man – it is his birth month – and I connect his countryside as best I can with our own. His hymn is painfully direct – 'The sick found health in his reply . . . yet he with troubles did remain.'

The Worshipper

Astonishing heat, greater than any since 1976, when my old pond completely dried up, the first time in living memory, and revealed its Victorian litter, muddy lamps, horse-chains, cracked crocks. The winds are like those on the African coast and carry a resinous air which coats everything with a kind of black honey. The grey churches are coolly welcoming and stand open for walkers and bikers. On Sundays a single holiday-maker adds conspicuously to the congregation. Xenophon, quoting Apollo, said that everyone's true worship was that which he found in use in the place where he chanced to be. This may have been all right for sacred groves and mountains, no doubt, but it would be putting one's charity to the test in some of today's churches.

I am moved by our small worshipping congregations, by the privacy of their public prayer, and by the impossibility of my ever knowing what is actually going on as they kneel, sit, stand, sing, say, dream. In service terms worship is that ultimate reverence which a community and an individual has to reactivate week after week. It must be familiar, even commonplace, and yet at the same time elevated and inspired. 'Wonder is the basis of worship,' said Carlyle. Wonder is unlikely to fill the entire act of worship, but I notice it creeping in here and there. Should it not, alas, alas. 'Religion . . . will glide out of mind,' warned Doctor Johnson, 'unless it be invigorated and re-impressed . . . by stated calls to worship.' I preach and teach on the text, 'The hour cometh, and now is, when the true worshippers shall worship the Father in spirit and truth.'

I remember once sitting in R. S. Thomas's church in North Wales with his poems in my head and his pulpit in my sight, the visitor from afar. I never confessed to it when we met in Ipswich to read our work in the Town Hall because I knew he hated prying. The God of the Old Testament never spoke once to poor old Eli, the saddest priest in scripture, the consecrated one who had never been granted 'the vision' nor understood silent prayer when a woman truly worshipped in his church. Church-going nowadays can be a traditional or pop concert *sans* worship. Yet who can prove its absence? No one – least of all myself as I too kneel, sit, stand, sing, say, dream in these ancient colonnades. One cannot always tell when something wonderful is going on.

Trinity Seven: St Mary Magdalene

This is the season of brief vanishings and of reappearances which now merit only the slightest enquiry. 'Did you have a good time?' Travel seems to be drained of wonder and stuffed with meals, with service, with airport tales. Gaudy photographs have become the voice of scenery. Myself in the classroom; 'Hands up all those who have been abroad.' Everybody. Yet the village retains many examples of true travel. There is Miss Beaumont, aged, formidable, who as a wartime nurse travelled to Burma and wrote a good book about it. But there is also young David who dashes now and then to Hong Kong, and young Mr C. who won't be back from Moscow in time to read his lesson. I think of those who lived in this house when the letter with the foreign stamp arrived, and the settling down as the voice of the son in New South Wales once more filled the room. Pages of scenery, a sentence or two about his health, the careful omission of homesickness. And all has to be well. Somehow the immensity of earthly distance is brought home to those who never leave home, who had what they called a day out. Pride and landscape jostled in such letters. But sometimes travel became all too much, all too hard. Newman wrote 'Lead, Kindly Light' because he had such a lonely, miserable time getting back to Oxford from the Mediterranean. Little Horkesley choir left Italy on Saturday night and were in their stalls on Sunday morning. 'Did you have a nice time?' Miss F., returning from Nepal, may have to miss the PCC.

British Legioners meet in the cricket pavilion and do not have to tell their travels, for these are written into them. Tobruk, the North Atlantic run, frightful jungles, Catterick. And like all villages, we have our not so very old Empire hands with, for me, riveting home movies of tea and rubber plantations, and of themselves so elegantly youthful. I myself now and then disappear, rarely for a holiday, although work in a foreign land becomes this in retrospect. The foreign land can as well be Hull as North Carolina. During either brief uprooting I glut on what I am seeing, where I am walking, taking everything in so that it will emerge on the page. I have to find a way to make the neighbours describe their journeys. My dread is the hunger-marcher with his smattering of Menu – today's second language – my plea is that he will put into his own words his first glimpse of the Tuscan hills. Isaiah says that wayfaring men, 'though fools', cannot miss the holy highway.

Trinity Eight: St James

C ombines are being lured from their barn-lairs, to fervent hopes that they will do their stuff. Will go. Although so modern, there is something neolithic in their huge, ponderous stroll across the field. Bernard, riding high, is lost in barley-dust. The poet John Clare practised his letters in such dust as a child, half-choking alongside his father in the threshing shed. Time to settle dates for our three harvest festivals, one for each parish. Woe betide he or she who thinks economically in terms of joint festivals. Alas, the harvests themselves are now among the least witnessed events in rural Britain. 'I see they are cutting by the river,' I tell a neighbour and am answered with a slight pause as he works it out. But great heat. It causes the house to stretch and groan. The garden bakes and Max cools under

rhubarb leaves. A yucca has sent up two feet of creamy bells with a faint scent straight from a Moorish palace.

At matins I speak on St Swithun whilst irrigation pipes drag water from the river and sprinkle it over the parched beet. He belongs to that vast congregation whose last wishes were flouted. 'Bury me where the raindrops will fall from the minster eave on to my grave. Lay me where friends *en route* to prayer will walk on me.' But soon they dug him up and enshrined him. One cannot afford to leave valuable assets lying in the

ground. After church we go to the Rix's farm for the annual
summer lunch, a properly gargantuan affair with raspberries
and all. The sun is by now under the mistaken belief that it is
shining on the Sudan. Home to hear that old (ninety-one) and
very dear Mrs Ambrose has that very hour died. She and her
son were having Sunday tea when she gave a tiny sigh and
departed, as they used to say, *this* life. She died in the house
where she was born. Congratulated on her true cottage garden,
a reproach to lawn-worshippers, she would say, 'I always think
that if you care for flowers they will come to you.' Whoever
was taking the service picked her up, driving her along the
lanes she walked as a girl. Only if the weather was atrocious
would she wave us on with the kind of not-today gesture she
might make to the milkman.

The Trinity Eight Collect with its 'never-failing providence'
has a Tudor harvest in sight. But it is its petition 'to put away
from us all hurtful things' which catches at the memory. I see
a parental hand gently but firmly opening my palm to remove
the sharp toy.

Graven Images

Hearing that Aldeburgh has declined to put up a statue to
Benjamin Britten reminded me of the two most influential
memorials in my young life. One was the fine statue to Gainsborough erected in Sudbury, the artist's birthplace, in 1913, a
gift from America, and the other was an obelisk set up by the
Catholic Fr. Hugh Rose at Hadleigh to the Protestant martyr

Dr Rowland Taylor on the spot where he was burnt in 1555. I very much doubt, had it been left to the councils of either of these Suffolk towns, that a penny would have been raised for such monuments. How they fascinated me – inspired me even. Dazzling Tom Gainsborough straddling our market-stalls; the bonfire site of the fat old Tudor rector who had, they said, transformed his parish into a little university. As a boy I dreamed of scholars and saints wandering around markets and cornfields, and of artists and poets sitting under trees. The absence of statues where statues should be never struck me. There was not one to the great John Constable who painted further up-river. I saw in Wales blush-making statues to 'philanthropists', i.e. coal and iron millionaires who let trickle a few pounds towards a gritty park where their semi-starved workforce could recreate.

When I lived in Aldeburgh, the only statue out in the open was to a brave dog. George Crabbe, that borough's critical genius, had been allowed a bust, but it was more or less tucked away out of sight in the north chapel of the parish church. It looks across to John Piper's window to Britten, and I now tend to think that the latter suffices. The composer's inescapable memorial is the sound the sea makes on the shingle, or up against concrete breakwaters, or as it sucks into the marshes.

The Church has notoriously disobeyed scripture with regard to statues. Both Leviticus and Paul are hotly against a 'standing image'. Jehovah promises good harvests and military victories to those who can resist a statue, and Paul reminds the new Christians that, each one of them being a temple to the living God, what need have they of images equivalent to those found in Graeco-Roman temples? Yet read Dame Felicitas Corrigan's splendid life of Helen Waddell and the spiritual enlightenment brought to this little girl, the daughter of Ulster missionaries in China, by the great Daibutsu of Kamakura, the largest bronze statue in the world, and puzzle again about standing images.

Had Helen not encountered every day this bronze serenity, she may never have found her way into that age of faith which smiles down on us from a thousand stone countenances in the old cathedrals.

The chief flowering of statues in our day is on war memorials. Robert Lowell could not bear them. Such monuments 'stick like a fishbone in the city's throat'.

Trinity Nine: Transfiguration of Our Lord

Matins, St Andrew's lofty and cool. Outside, burning tombs. John has managed three hours' baling before tidying himself up and sitting in his customary place. The lessons are lengthy – a fascinating one about Jeremiah presenting the king with a book which the latter couldn't bear to publish, so he cut it up with his penknife and threw it, leaf by leaf, on the fire. It strikes twelve before the last hymn, an event at Wormingford which sends a *frisson* of panic through the congregation, though why I have never discovered. Perhaps they were all brought up on *Cinderella*. However, it is I who have to catch a train – to Dorchester for the Thomas Hardy Conference. Sunday cricket matches speed by every few miles. I reread my lecture and tell myself that's that. Too late for second thoughts. It is about Hardy and John Clare, 'A Soil Observed, a Soil Ploughed'. In less than twelve hours I am in 'Mellstock', or Stinsford as the signposts call it.

It is here that I think of meditating children, of boys and

girls abstracting faith and faithlessness from what surrounds them as the service drones on. Whole tracts of liturgy pass unnoticed as their wandering, wondering glances take in carved words, tall arches, filtered light. We have all done it. Church-going for infants takes them to later indescribable destinations. 'I'm not asleep; I'm thinking.' 'Then sit up straight; I won't tell you again.' Mercifully it has never been the duty of rectors to lean over their pulpits with a 'Stop that day-dreaming, boy!' And thus, when we are young and wide awake, we fall to speculation as to what it all means, this vast room in which you have to kneel. When Tom Hardy sat here his bird-eye marvelled about a florid memorial in the north aisle to a gentleman named Angel Grey. Now read on, as they say. Further seeds for what was to come are everywhere. Outside, his 'Gurgoyles' leer down, only waiting for the weather to break in order to provide for the new dead the most desolating fate for them which only he could imagine, rain pouring on their graves. Under my feet, beneath the hot grass, lies the most famous silenced choir in English literature. On a storm-coloured window are Hardy's favourite scriptural sentences, those which end with, 'and after the fire a still small voice'.

This is the voice which Samuel the Temple child heard so distinctly. There is a notion – an insistence – that the worshipping child has to comprehend everything that happens in church. But who does? Like him or her, let us stare about us.

Death of a Young Farmer

Getting the balance right might be thought admirable, though not in every quarter. Balance is too equable, too lacking in drama. Many in the countryside prefer it when things are way out or at rock bottom. We have our doomsayers, both male and female. A new enterprise starts up in the village – 'I give it till Christmas.' A long time ago, after I had written about the great agricultural depression, an old farmer's wife beckoned me; 'My dear, you should have come to me. I could have told you much worse than that!' I delight in our doomsayers and would never think of attempting to balance their blackness with a spot of rational light. The pleasures of misery, let them not be denied.

But real darkness hangs in our little firmament as still-young people die. Friends who were seen in the fields until just the other day. We say their names formally in church and tenderly to ourselves every day of the week. Have we ever been more medical and less philosophical about death? How I detest the neologism 'terminal illness' and hope that when my time comes and they ask after me, the reply will be, 'He is dying.' These serious thoughts arise when one has to balance the rural idyll with sad realities common to us all. We are some 800 souls all told in the united benefice – the smallest in the diocese – and small changes and profound departures cast a kind of universal shadow across the valley. At the Bell-Sunday service I reminded them of the passing-bell – the one which John Donne mentions – and which was heard in the village until 1914, when the farmworkers in the fields would straighten up and count the strokes. Seventy-two, seventy-three . . . 'He had a good innings.' Or twenty-five, twenty-six, then silence.

I meet the ringers in the Crown, David, Bernard, Christopher,

Evelyn, all brown as berries and clearly immortal. Their cars glitter in the yard. Ringers are masters of continuity. No sooner do old hands leave hold of the ropes than young hands catch on. We talk of Cecil Pipe the great Suffolk ringer, now with God. He once told me that it was 'the parson's daughters who started me off'. He had watched them raise the bell and when they had disappeared, tried it himself. He was twelve. He said, 'You must bring these two things together in your mind and let them rest there for ever, bells and time, and bells and time . . .'

A tunicked St Alban looks down from his position on the reredos. Suffered *c.* 209 on a hilltop in June, a young Romano-Briton. The children like him and are sad for him. 'What was the hill called?' 'Holmhurst Hill.'

Trinity Ten

Summer lightning. It throws the trip-switch and the old rooms resume their darkness. Or rather an intermittent brilliance. Enormously brave or daft, I stroll up the track to where it rises and I can see, miles off, Stoke-by-Nayland tower which Marjorie has had floodlit especially for her grandson's birthday. As boys, my brother and I would climb its cold stairs to confirm whether indeed a waggon-and-horses could be turned on its leads, or whether you could see Harwich Water. Now here it is, framed in ash trees, a still flame among the on—off agitation of the universe.

Such vividness set by, the village at this moment can only

be described as being in a state of pause. Lots of people are 'away' – they don't call it holiday. 'We shall be away', and the dates. An elaborate silence announces that the school is away. The combines are certainly away, having done the barley and not being able to cut the corn for another fortnight at least. Rain falls across the latter in sheets, in torrents, hissing as it hits the dry ears and rock-soil. I am solicitous about this when I meet Mr William Brown who, approaching his century, sits in his car looking out, both motionless. Won't it harm the harvest? Not a bit. It will fatten it up. Just what was wanted. I tell him about the lit tower because he can now not see that far.

It has been a week of much ecclesiastical hissing one way or another. Such drama and reporters having to brush-up their Anglicanism. I remember once reading about the nation-shaking religious debates of Victorian Britain, and the writer saying that we would never see their like again. Well this one is very like and the papers are full of it, the more popular the fuller. I myself have heard Voices saying 'Have you considered your position?' Do seekers have a position, I mean a leg to stand on? Or only finders? Where do seekers stand? Should they seek out the finders or someone else? It is an interesting question to put to summer lightning. Duncan's sheep cluster on the rim of the hill, alternately seen and unseen, and I hope not frightened by drum-rolls of distant thunder. Pheasants crash about uneasily although every other kind of bird seems to be 'away'. Travelling through this neon-sign of a night, I think of that great scriptural word 'seek'. Discovering Christ in a secret place they told him 'All men seek for thee.' Shakespeare says, 'Light seeking light doth light of light beguile.' Young George Fox stood on Pendle and saw stretching before him the country of the Seekers. It was that he – and they – found what they were searching for.

In the Vestry

Never so many waiting starlings. Were there five wires linking my transformer to Maltings Farm they would have sat there like some opening movement of a great piece of music. The mood is one of impending profligacy. Notices are being fixed to the roadside to warn drivers where the grain-wagons will turn in or emerge. It is very still. They are waiting to cut. Any day now the towering machines will, with a bit of luck, clank from the dens in which they have been sleeping these last fifty weeks and the wheat-dust will fly.

I have always loved waiting. Not too long, of course. Waiting for the friend to appear and who should be neither late nor early, so as not to spoil the waiting with anxiety or prevent there being a wait at all. Ditto with trains. Not to catch them by the skin of one's teeth or to have to stand on the platform for an hour, losing patience and losing heart. Just a nice wait so that one can look through the waiting-room window at the familiar meadows which cover King Cymbeline's city. Every priest will know about that special wait before the service begins. The bell is going, the cars are still arriving, the clock is ticking, the vestry prayer has been whispered, the church door has opened and closed heaven knows how many times, and still he must wait. And how pleasant it is. Another four minutes to read the framed Table of Fees, or to muse on the Victorian clergy in the framed photographs, with their huge snowy collars and resting hands – to think of them standing where he is standing, just waiting for the service to begin. 'Prepare us, O God, for the worship of Thine house.'

Our three vestries are distinctive where waiting is concerned. Little Horkesley's is ebullient, lots of choir finding lots of music and waiting for even more choir to finish ringing, and for the last-minuter to rush in at the penultimate moment. 'Don't hurry, plenty of time!' This is not so, but one has to be Christian in the circumstances. My mother was always late for church, something she always denied, declaring 'They started early.' Which was one way of looking at it. At Wormingford the waiting is for the congregation *en masse*. A minute to eleven and the church is empty and then, just as the clock is about to strike, there they all are in their proper places. It is a miracle. They are last-minuters, a special race, and by every law of rush they should be out of puff, but they are unhurried. They kneel and sit and exchange little leisurely greetings. And there is still a full thirty seconds to go. Alone in Mount Bures vestry, the waiting is an enchantment. I have often had a good mind to ask God to let old Mr Chaplin toll on for ever, or to the end of our days, whichever is the longest.

On the Village Bus

August for the traveller. In church I paraphrase St Paul's complicated journey from Caesarea to Rome. It took him months and scarcely a creak of the *Castor and Pollux* is missing from the narrative. And that 'uncommon kindness' of the Maltese when they ran his ship ashore in the pouring rain. And then that long walk to Rome on the Appian Way, and the Christians there hurrying out to meet him. Everyone listens intently. It is a classic traveller's tale. I return to find the old green lane which swoops down to the house broadened into a grand highway to the corn. Bernard has ceremoniously laid low

its overgrowth with the 'murderer' or hedge-cutter, and the partridges are out in state.

My August travels include a trip on the village bus to Bury St Edmunds, which might well be described as autobiography via public transport. For the bus winds through some twenty miles of my existence, taking in both old roads and new roads, making short cuts through the farmland and picking up vaguely familiar passengers. There is the church in which I sang, there is the church of my baptism and, in the long grass somewhere behind it, the grandparents' graves. And there, dotted all over the high ground, are the churches against which I propped my bike, a teenage postulant of 'the crew/That tap and jot and know what rood-lofts were'. They all rise from their appointed places once more to dominate the Suffolk harvest. And there, hurrying by, are grandfather's fields, now set aside and bobbing with rooks, and the drifts where he ran his sheep. And there mighty Holy Trinity, Long Melford, stares over three miles to equally mighty St Peter and St Paul, Lavenham, where as children we climbed the tower, desperately praying not to be locked in by the verger, so that our bones would be discovered by the ringers months hence and justly used by the rector as an object lesson on trespass. Forgive us our trespass, dear old Lavenham man. 'Come you down!' he'd shout. But up, up, up, we went to faint cries of, 'Then be careful!' And there was the entire world spread out like a toy and the huge tower apparently asway from our weight. Forgive a history-mad boy for so much poking and prying among sacred things and rarely if ever obeying the pretty card pinned on the door – 'Say a prayer for yourself and those who worship here.'

Girls in long skirts and boys with Henry V haircuts climb aboard. Sixth-form lovers. They drink from a cardboard box using the same straw, and drop off in consecutive villages. The old woman who reads novels is with us. Sometimes the driver waits for her to finish her page as, confused by romance and his speed, she alights, her face still enchanted with fiction.

Trinity Eleven

Outside there being what the Proverbs calls 'a continual dropping in a very rainy day', I am inside browsing, a nice word which equally applies to Mr Knighton's sheep. They are Welsh mules, or hybrids, and they are munching their way through the aftermath, or the new growth which follows the haymaking. The rainy day has turned them into perambulating sponges, although they don't seem to mind, it being warm. Having some time in hand, I dip into this and that until, suddenly, I am deep once more in Colette's sublime *Earthly Paradise*. No longer am I by the Stour, but on the banks of the Yonne in the 1880s. And I can hear the novelist's mother shouting 'Look!' – her perennial command. Keep your eyes open, girl, boy, grown man and woman. I read about Colette and her mother, Sido, that August, an imperially named month which brings the first withering and darkening of plants. The first ripening too. Vast tangles of convolvulus, hogweed and seeded grass tower in my ditches. This is the growth called 'rubbish' in the village. 'You want to get rid of that rubbish.' Do I? Colette writes, 'An infallible memory guides my recollections through the tangled garden of my infancy.'

'What a memory you have!' some of the villagers say, but without envy. Better to forget things. Particularly the tangles. Strangely, Proverbs' dropping rain seems not to drench the corn, which continues its dry rustle. But now and then, when there is an extra hard downpour, it hisses like spit on a hob. Lots of damp butterflies.

One of the writer's tasks is to point out the sights as life jogs along. Look! Also to follow with his eyes a pointing finger and to respond to another's 'Look!' Walking through summer rain is a kind of treat; I make my way to a pan-sized mushroom which shines in the meadow. Some words from a mid-August collect turn over in my head – that we are not 'sufficient' of ourselves to think anything of ourselves. What a relief. Returning, I think of Michael Ramsey's little book *Be Still and Know* and find what I am looking for. It is where he calls meditation a deliberate use of silence. Writers use a great deal of silence, and deliberately. How I wish that my memory of this book had been infallible when I spoke to its author in a Cambridge garden, the only time we met. Instead, he told me how he used to bicycle through Suffolk in August, adding, 'Long ago. I forget what we were looking for.' Not the right words, for certain; he was never at a loss for these. And so back to Colette and her rain-pitted pond, and pleased by the truthfulness of things.

The Winged Ones

L onged-for rains are on their way and the fatuous weather-
man on the radio warns us of 'the wet stuff'. He would be more respectful could he see the deep fissures in the fields and the river running low. The air is throbbing with a dozen combine harvesters as the farmers hurry to get the barley and wheat in before what we all hope will be a proper soaking. There was a week during the last few baking days when the countryside became winged. Painted Ladies had arrived from North Africa in their many thousands. So had everyone's bees from miles around, so had countless moths. They included many shining Silver Y moths, so called because they wear this

letter on their backs. Naturally, the flycatchers flew in to make the most of this manna from heaven. Such a glinting, shimmering collective of wings as had not been seen for years. The Painted Ladies set up court on the convolvulus bank, creating a brilliant living canopy over the pink flowers which we as children called lamps. I, of course, spoke to Mr Harley about this butterfly phenomenon – we have an authority on almost anything you like to mention – and he told me, 'Yes, the Painted Ladies had indeed flown over from North Africa to sit in the sun on our thistle-heads.'

But it was the myriad wingedness which entranced us all. Such a multiplicity of flight by birds, insects, seeds there was all at once as to make humanity feel grounded – unless one went to Stansted, of course. Else the entire valley was airborne. What will happen when it rains? Will the winged courts take shelter? All those gauzy creatures finding shelter, the Ladies, the Emperors, the Whites, the Blues, the Silver Y moths, the darting flycatchers, beneath the summer leaves.

Religion is filled with flight and longings for flight. It has a winged language which alights on the earth but which cannot be earth-bound, even at its most earthy. David saw his God astride a cherub on the wings of the wind, a thrilling sight. Inherent long before then in human thinking was the conviction that not only cherubim would ride the wind. Men too. One of these mortal days. Until then one had to make do with angels. Frequently in the medieval imagination the angel was less God's messenger than a man doing what he knew he should be able to do – fly. Though never of course from God, for what was the use? 'If I take the wings of the morning . . . to the uttermost parts . . . Thou art there.' George Herbert's 'pattern poem' *Easter Wings* is shaped like an angel's wings in descent, as it were from a butterfly's wings. I think of the sick priest flying along on his horse to Old Sarum for fresh air when Bemerton was sticky and close. 'O let me rise as larks, harmoniously,/

And sing this day thy victories/Then shall the fall further the flight in me.'

Trinity Twelve: St Bartholomew

Late summer on the calendar, early autumn on the ground. The harvest is in and its aftermath begins to flourish on the stubble. The cracked fields look as though they haven't been rained on for a year. Their dust films our shoes as we set out on the annual farm walk. The King's Farm bullocks shake their heads as the congregation threads its way across their pasture and up a great meadow to Vicky's, where, as though we had crossed the Sahara, lemonade awaits us. Some of them are acres ahead and the carrying talk reminds me of the calling conversations held by farmworkers many years ago, or by fishermen in their midnight boats. Little Horkesley at three on a Sunday afternoon is equally becalmed, equally loquacious. Lines from an Addison hymn jumble around in my head, such as 'When in the sultry glebe I faint' and 'Through devious lonely wilds I stray'. Why they should when we are all full of Sunday dinner and footpath maps I can't imagine. Through Vicky's tall wood where every tree reaches for the skies, over the stripped pea fields, past the reservoir and across the lane to Knight's Farm and an astonished chorus by calves, guinea fowl, cockerels and other creatures at this invasion. Is there to be no rest? The walk has taken us through the ancient growing landscape of Crabb's, Knowles's, Breewood Hall, Vinesse and Hay Farms.

During tea Mr Knighton brings me two letters to his great-grandfather from S. Wesley and I read them by the barn. At six we move to a lawn set out with straw-bales and sing evensong. Vicky reads Ruth 2, and I give an impromptu sermon on the Lord's ancestry, which all began in that Bethlehem harvest field – Bethlehem 'the House of Bread'. We sing the evening hymn and the animals join in. There are forty of us. Unless there is some acquaintance with the fields, why live in the country? How worship in a village church?

Trinity Thirteen

Worked on my book all the morning. Gather William pears, or Williams's pears, to be didactic, as they are named after a Mr Williams who was the first person to distribute Bon Chrétien pears in England. They are the palest gold with rough dark freckling, and delicious beyond words. Grey squirrels shake the hazel stands, leaping about at sky level, and aggravating Max the cat, who finds them quite unbearable. He clicks his teeth at their antics, a gesture of his utmost displeasure. Indoors, I pay homage to a slate clock with a good tick and bad timing. Topped by a brass sphinx, it is always slow, but what a classy sound. This is a *c.* 1850 clock kept for its philosophical voice. When I forget to wind it, the silence is that of my heart missing beats.

Diana Collins arrives at six and takes me to supper at the Crown. I love the way her talk moves so eagerly from the parochial to the universal, and back again, with never a severing of the links. Her and John Collins's faith has been so acted upon where the great moral issues of the post-war years were concerned as to make my own faithfulness almost fugitive in comparison. Tonight we talk 'shop' re the books we are currently writing. The news of the Israeli–Palestinian *rapprochement* casts a glow, although so extraordinary that we both feel that we have a right to a little incredulity. Whatever next? The two Irelands? Who knows? There, as here, the people and their politicians are gapingly apart. Diana and I talk about Jericho, Palestine's new capital. Jericho, where blind Bartimeus threw off his cloak, the faster to run towards that voice, that giver of Sight. The resonance of such towns in Christian ears, their millennial utility. During the 1950s, Kathleen Kenyon dug deep in Jericho and found 'civitas' at a time when Abraham was still living in a tent.

I witness the marriage of two friends in a Registry Office, the first time I have been inside one. The building itself is 1960s Georgian and the office everybody's front room. The surroundings are puzzlingly *déjà vu* until it all comes back to me. We are in the great timber-yard where the creamy boards of oak, ash, elm (coffin and floor wood) and walnut lay seasoning, and the sawpits sang. Now the Registry Office and other discreet amenities are to be discovered there. The Registrar and his clerk arrive and my friends are married in what seems like five minutes. We are assured that the room we are in has been 'solemnized'. We face a mottled grey wall. Behind us are coloured photographs of Suffolk and some artificial flowers. Everything is spick and span. The lady with the register writes and writes. The Registrar borrows our camera to photograph us. Marriage lines are presented to the bride, who is enormously elegant in black. We return to champagne and smoked salmon and a lovely brandified cake. 'Did you notice,' asks the groom 'that there was a "thee"?' I was actually moved by these legal requirements, and by the Registrar's efforts to breathe some sense of occasion into them.

John Bunyan

The government's White Paper on rural Britain appears and so do young BBC newsmen with hand-held cameras. Questions, questions. We all have our say and friends telephone from far and wide saying, 'We saw you!' I held forth on the need to keep local craftsmen in their native places, and not have them forced to find housing far from home, whilst incomers buy up their barns and cottages. Craftsmen are a cantankerous breed, as we know, but happy is the village which still contains their groans. I stick up for Simon the carpenter who replaced my old sash window with a perfect new old sash window. His people have lived here for a century, his parents run the farm shop and he employs half a dozen excellent wood-workers. So he must stay.

The White Paper cannot bridge the gap – the chasm – which has opened between the village 'then' and the village 'now'. Peggy brings me a sepia photograph of sugar-beeting in 1933. Ten poor men in muddy sacks – 'Dad on the extreme right, grand-dad third from left'. Far from elderly folk see themselves in similar positions. They shake their heads. They can't 'puzzle it out'. Such near old times, such bad old days. In the evening I watch D. H. Lawrence's *The Widowing of Mrs Holroyd* on television. It is intensely moving – that washing the pit-dirt from the young body by wife and mother. A *pietà*. But the actors do not know how to light an oil lamp or fold sheets. Walking in Cornwall some years ago I came to the epic slate pit of Delabole, the immense hole from which half the roofs of Britain originated. And there, dressed like his grandfather and surrounded by tourists, sat a solitary figure splitting and sizing slates. This was my initiation to theme-park Britain.

But there are all the rural pluses. Rambling and cycling are on the increase. Film has revolutionized natural history, and thus much rural behaviour. We watch more, destroy less. As for gardening! God walks in the cool of the evening in countless Edens. Dame Julian was right. Christ and Everyman were to be as one in the service of God. Christ and man were 'to be a gardener, digging and banking, toiling and sweating, turning and trenching the ground, watering the plants the while'. And by 'keeping at this work he would make sweet streams to flow and fine abundant fruits to grow, and bring them to his Lord'. I suppose the question is, how is one to become a servant of God – not to mention one's neighbours – in today's country-side? How does one get out of the theme-park into the reality? Walking to the vicarage to arrange the services with Michael, I stopped to chat to Maisie in her lovely garden. She is cutting nerines to place on Anne's grave. 'They should have gone by now' – she means certain flowers.

Veterans: VJ Day

An unusual week, with the generation game being played for all it is worth. Due to us all living so long it has become the common experience to have four, rather than three, tiers of relations flourishing side by side. But the cultural distinctions seem more apparent than ever. After Arthur's funeral, we took refreshment in the schoolroom where he had once sat, learning by rote, making hooked letters with his slate-pencil. This before 1914. Now his computer-literate great-grandchildren crowd into the corners, stuffing sandwiches, and too small to mourn. Arthur's new widow sits at a table, delicately pretty at ninety and, so far as anyone can tell, neither sad nor troubled. When I take her hands in mine, they are as fine as flowers. She offers the ghost of a smile. We left the grave-digger sunbathing by the hedge. Roman tiles in the church walls were being fired all over again by the Sahara heat, and papery leaves were scuttling along the grass paths. I had read, 'The days of our age and threescore years and ten; and though men be so strong, that they come to fourscore years . . .' and had noted two of Arthur's contemporaries turn to one another and grin. Shall we not soon be saying, 'Poor so-and-so has gone – and him only eighty!'

At the VJ Service there were few present under fifty, although the church was packed. 'Why should there be?' is what I asked myself. We all trooped into the sports pavilion afterwards, where the bar was crowded with youngsters hungry for football after the languors of cricket. They received us bashfully and we might, trailing as we did the experiences of Kohima, the Western Desert and Battle of Britain skies, have marched in straight from the Crimea for all they could understand or share. They shrank politely away from all the dark suits and medals. Soon they were running across the pitch, ignoring the crease and wheeling the goal-posts into position, whilst a waning harvest moon climbed from behind the trees to challenge our flaring beacon. The VJ service, as such official occasions sometimes do, had moved from adequacy to poignancy. And yet, as Paul pointed out, it was *our* tomorrow for whom the Kohima dead had given their today – not the tomorrow of those still unborn. How can any of us know what such tomorrows are? With nightly horrors on our evening screen, what was so special about the cruelties of the Burma Road? the village footballers might ask. Looking at them, I realize that none was as youthful as Arthur when he married his Beatrice at the beginning of the brief peace.

Trinity Fourteen: Nativity of the Blessed Virgin Mary

O more than happy countryman, I have just discovered that Bottengoms Farm fills the requirements of Horace's prayer – 'a piece of land not so very large, which would contain a garden, and near the house a spring of ever-flowing water, and beyond these a bit of wood'. Roy Chapman our house agent couldn't go far wrong with that.

A letter from the Records Office. Please may our registers be microfilmed for the Genealogical Society of Utah? Yes, the writer of Chronicles would have said. No, would have been St Paul's reply. I will explain anon. Meanwhile I search them pretty regularly for correspondents. They make good reading even if there are rather a lot of characters, as somebody complained of the telephone directory. The handwriting itself enchants me. I look for the Reverend Mr Pilgrim's, 'an honest but weakly man' who in late August 1644 died in the pulpit. The psalm for his death-day was number thirty – 'Thou has turned for me my mourning into dancing . . . and girded me with gladness.' Outside, it being a puritan sabbath, there would have been silence in the same half-harvested fields.

But ancestry. Some of the neighbours are well into it, for it is an intoxicant. It was once part of religion. The Jews were heavily committed to it and the Gospels open fair and square with Christ's family-tree. 'All Israel was reckoned by genealogies' says Chronicles. St Paul would have none of it. Writing to young Timothy he says, 'Neither give heed to tables and endless genealogies'. Writing to young Titus, he advises, 'Avoid foolish questions and genealogies'. My post frequently contains questions whose answers can only be found among the births, marriages and deaths – and found quickly, were it not for the fact that these absorbing handwritten 'trees' belonging to the bit of wood which is Wormingford simply will not let me go. Now and then an Elizabethan or Georgian vicar adds a little extra, or is distressingly plain – 'bastard'. But the inks, the pens, the signatories to our rites of passage, how I stare into them. At Monewden, Suffolk, where I used to take matins, the church-wardens always wrote-in the weather – 'Bad gale', '80 in the shade', 'Snow, no service'. Last Sunday I should – there is a column for it – enter my text. In our ancestral registers I should have written that I preached about Bartholomew who, as his hymn bleakly puts it, 'is nothing but a name'.

An old miller once asked me, 'Did you hear the tempest last night?' Up at six to find that there had been far more tempest on the BBC's charts than in our valley. Delicate poppies caught what there was of it and sprawl in their beds like drenched taffeta. I review some natural history books and then walk to

Wormingford church. It is our turn to be host to the Deanery for the yearly 'Quiet'. It is the Nativity of Mary and the theme of these devotions is total obedience to God and its historic consequences. Our vicar John Larter leads them from the chancel step. Huge silences engulf us. As I suffer, if this is the word, from an almost uncontrollable state of dream, it becomes quite an effort for me to use these silences for wordless prayer. I find myself contrasting the quietness of this ancient interior out of service-time with the created quietness of us all at this moment. The Rural Dean plays the organ. Owls call. I am mentally half in a sonorous Stuart hymn and half in Rilke's 'Annunciation', one of my favourite poems from his *Picture Book*. Rilke's anger seems to have taken in some Renaissance paintings on his way to the Virgin. He is also rather like a child who, having carried a message a long distance, needs to get his breath back before delivering it.

> 'I'm but a breeze within the wood,
> you, Lady, are the Tree.'

Trinity Fifteen

Trinity Fifteen and our Flower and Vegetable Show. I am allowed to judge the Children's Section. Real judges come from afar with clean hands and fastidious requirements. I shall not forget their dismissal of my potatoes for having 'mixed colours'. The village hall smells of chrysanthemums and ambition. The trophies shine. For anyone interested in a modest immortality I recommend the giving of a silver cup, deeply engraved with one's generosity, to the annual flower show. It is a blowy day and exhibitors struggle from cars with their entries. The tables are all set neatly and covered with snowy lining paper. Enormous marrows are out but gargantuan blooms are in. Late roses pose singly in pretty vases. Colonel Easten and Mr Brown keep order. As well as the show, there is a wedding and the yearly Bike Ride to raise funds for the churches. Some people are involved in all three pursuits, with big problems about what to wear.

I remain haunted by the Debach and Boulge Show where I had to take the awards from the treasurer and hand them to the winners, a pair of ancient rivals who fought each other for the most cups and the most cash so fiercely that it was hard for the rest of us to get a look in. Our seat of custom was in Edward FitzGerald's little house – 'Look to the blowing Rose about us' – and I could hear his voice, 'like a cricket ball with a break in it', someone said, and could sense his presence. A friend called him 'the Prince of Quietists . . . his tranquillity is like a pirated copy of the peace of the peace of God.' Whilst the winners gloated over their takings, both of them so laden with trophies that they looked like burglars, I would glance across the churchyard hedge where our Irish-Suffolk poet rested beneath a rose from Omar's tomb. Edward FitzGerald always wore his thickest coat in church 'as fungi grow in great numbers about the communion table'. This was in 1843 when 'parson and clerk got through the service see-saw like two men in a sawpit'. He had a blackboard set up in the nave and taught the villagers to read music. And so he went on, 'reading a little, drawing a little, playing a little, smoking a little' and writing a great deal – mostly glorious letters. They – the ancestors of the flower-show folk – thought him very odd, but as his grave reminded them 'It is He that hath made us, and not we ourselves.' But back to Wormingford and its laden trestles and

the aromatic hall, and the unconcealed bliss of winning Colonel Lucas's silver rose-bowl. *Exultate Deo.*

The autumn equinox = 'equal night'. Old Sir Thomas Browne, of whom I am an addict, musing over prehistory, which was a black hole in his day, wrote, 'The night of time far surpasseth the day, and who knows when was the equinox?' It has been very unequal weather and autumn and St Matthew arrived together in a wild state. First tempests, as the old people still call them and then that late hot sunshine which ripens fruit by the hour. Sir Thomas aside, I have as my prime-the-pump book the *Diaries* of Sylvia Townsend Warner. I always start the morning with a writer who can get me going. This week she is at her equinoctial best as she wakes up to feel old and then goes to her window to see 'such a glory of stars, solitary, unfrequented, secure, *and yet transient*, that I cried out, "In wisdom hast thou made them all", and slept again, comforted by that enormous transience'.

The longish walk to the village shop, more as an outing between pages than to buy something, for it delivers in its meticulous way all that I require. I note enough food *en route* to feed me until October, sudden mushrooms, wet blackberries, bullaces, nuts, avalanches of falls. At the shop Margaret and her son show their customary surprise when I enter, my address conferring as it does hermit status. The next village, Bures, used to have a store owned by a Mr Harrod, and friends there would say, 'Well, we get everything we need from Harrod's,' and went up in the world with those not in the know. What with Margaret's shop and my laden garden, I can cross the supermarket off my list.

St Matthew's collect contains a favourite finger-wagging word – 'inordinate'. It is getting at the apostle's past as a taxman. Not for us covetous desires and inordinate love of riches. Nor for us inordinate affection, although quite how one is to keep

this within bounds I have failed to understand. Some friends, the cat, some books, this landscape familiar to me since boyhood, are all in receipt of my inordinate affection and the cat would not be pleased with anything less. But if I am not covetous, it is because I have all I need. So no virtue in this. The epistle is far from equinoctial. No equality of night and light there. Light reigns. The autumn days are days to savour. There is a sweet rot in the air. Grey squirrels are allowed to do what we must not do, lay up treasure in the earth.

A four-mile walk along the river. It winds between the counties in alternating stretches of unruffled surface and splashing glitter, one reach a glassy path for young swans, the next a watery turmoil for young canoeists. East Anglian Baptists were 'taken under' such local rivers for generations, usually on warm summer evenings, with all their friends singing on the bank.

St Matthew

The ploughs have gone in – and gone home. The landscape is brown and lined like an old face. Brisk rains have blunted the sharp furrows. In no time all will be green with winter wheat. I preached on Matthew, the equinoctial apostle, about his being called from his calling. Matthew the taxman in the garrison town. Being autumn, I am called to take stock of the papery retreat which is my study, to tip out the crammed files and give notice to the fat harvest spiders. Below, in the wet garden, cyclamen and naked ladies flaunt themselves in social groups, and bedraggled pheasants strut about in pairs. At dusk there is a majestic swish of wings as echelons of geese make for the river. Aeronautics have demoted somewhat the wonder of wings, whether of birds or of angels. Natural (eagle's) and supernatural (cherub's) wings are first mentioned in Exodus, the book of flight. As the Bible proceeds they become emblems of soaring power or of comfort and protection. Matthew alone mentions Christ's wing metaphor – 'How often would I have gathered thy children together, even as a hen gathereth her chickens under her wings, and ye would not!' I am reading the very near unbearable biography of Gerard Manley Hopkins and of course I reread his glorious *Windhover*, a kestrel poem dedicated 'to Christ our Lord'. But oh the horror that his religion should have forced him to hide his marvels from the eyes of his superiors. Any authority, whether religious or secular, which stifles its writers diminishes itself.

The jolt of seeing a poet one knew on the obituary page, this time Donald Davie, master of Christian irony. We once had to judge the George Crabbe poetry competition and he would telephone from Exeter to add or subtract from the shortlist, but never when it was the last without bringing my attention to some redemptive verse or line. We announced the winners in Aldeburgh Church, standing by the bust of Crabbe, and sensing that bitter genius's ears alert to our every word. There was the Jacobean pulpit from which he preached, below roared his treacherous sea. My first – youthful – church-wardenship was at Great Glemham, one of the poet–parson's livings, and where on January afternoons he would take even-song until he could no longer see the book, then snap it shut and cry, 'All go home!' I told Donald Davie this tale. He gave me his *To Scorch or Freeze* poems which begin with his version of Psalm 39 –

> I held my tongue, I said nothing;
> no, not comfortable words.
> 'Writing-block', it's called;

– most discomforting, in fact.

Trinity Sixteen

People have often been condemned for taking the parochial view of life, although this could not have been entirely possible even during the past, when what was occurring in the next county could be as irrelevant as what was going on in Africa. Yet news from afar would have sometimes breached the parish defences. Thomas Hardy said that his grandmother was ironing her best muslin gown when the news broke in that Marie Antoinette had been executed. 'She put down her iron, and stood still, the event so greatly affecting her mind.' I get up before dawn these short days and do not stand still, not even when the news is of hundreds drowning. Instead, as murder follows ferry sinkings, then political chicaneries follow murder, and the intractabilities of Ireland and Bosnia are spelt out for the thousandth time, I put on the kettle and feed the cat. Our hunter–gatherer is the newsman and what he brings home to us is far more than we can cope with. An emotional and intelligent response to disaster – or to triumph – would appear to rely upon some aspect of a shared culture, and preferably one not too far away. There are mornings when I try to take it all in, and mornings when I twist aside, like a child facing a full spoon.

My father thought that even a black December morning was the best time of the day. Earliness suits me too. I can hear myself tick. But not if I switch-on. Then, if I am honest, I can hear very little. At matins and evensong I make a habit of bringing the worst and the best of what news hunter–gatherers have fed into me, out into the open, in the petitionary prayers drawing our own and God's attention to this week's horrors and blessings. My message is that we must not be withdrawn into our own village concerns but must think of India or

London, or some such out of the way place, and not be introverted or narrow or whatever. And the congregation, many of whom travel miles all the week and are stuffed with terrors and shortcomings by television each evening, agrees. It won't do to turn our backs on what is happening in the great world.

Chance would be a fine thing, I tell myself as the garden lightens and the sun peers through the mist in its short-sighted fashion, and Max twirls his tail at the effrontery of the bullfinches just the other side of the pane, and who are calmly breakfasting on eryngo seedheads not a yard from his whiskers. The new morning feeds me its specific joy and the radio, should it be on, a generalized sorrow.

Trinity Seventeen

Heady days for those of us who live in a marine climate. For in early autumn magnificent clouds parade across the firmament, a ceaseless panorama of aerial alps and rosy canyons, floating towers and beckoning cities of which neither peak nor pinnacle can maintain its shape for more than a few seconds. The dream-like legato of the September skies drags me along with it. A harvest-moon stares frankly into the house with a 'Here I am once more, but where are the sights I used to see, the tired field-men, the thankful supper, the tithes and quarter-rent on the scrubbed table?' But the clouds travel on in a moving frieze behind the ash trees. The heavens roll from yellow to pink, or to just plain gold as the moon fancies. Such skies! Whether it be day or night. The bedridden woman cannot take her eyes off them. They are her transport now. 'They are better than the pictures – they take me out of myself.'

Chinese businessmen used to invite a few friends back to clouds and a drink after a hard day in the counting-house. Freshly robed, they would sit on the terrace in silence and allow cloud patterns to fill their heads for an hour or so. No one was permitted to comment, as we did as children, 'There's a giant! There's an elephant!' One must eventually make a grown-up response to clouds. The bedridden woman said that in her opinion they were much neglected. She meant as natural objects which had the power to get the spirit moving. I was reminded of David's song of gratitude in II Kings 22 in which God and a cherub ride the wings of the wind like a monarch in a Rubens apotheosis, creating, as David says, dark pavilions all around them. Making weather, no less. Both black and lit pavilions scud above the roof-tops, firing my windows and then sailing on to ignite the church tower.

John Constable, who painted just over the hill, and whose uncle ground the Wormingford corn and carried on his barges the Wormingford coals, was much outside in autumn – cloud-catching. He told his sceptical contemporaries that where landscape was concerned, it was the sky which provided what he called 'the keynote'. Although most artists then had a rural background, this obvious fact never previously crossed their minds. But Constable had read a book called *The Climate of London* by Luke Howard, the proto-weatherman, and had undergone cloud conversion. So had Goethe, so had Shelley. Howard had done the impossible. He had given names to vapour, lovely names such as cirrus, cumulus, stratus and nimbus – rain-clouds. And so doing he had not only educated the poets and artists, but founded a career for Michael Fish. 'It is clouding over,' remarks Mrs Burge for something neighbourly to say. We are old friends and we do not have to tax our brains.

Lancelot Andrewes † 1626

Warm, blustering winds and tumbling fruit. The river's surface crinkles under the attack and weathervanes spin around. Crows and gulls are blown into each other's air-space, and there is all the usual October exultation. The wildness and a procession of harvest festivals remind me of visits to Morwenstow, Parson Hawker's autocratic kingdom, and watching the Cornish sea dashing itself against his limits. They said he commanded his parishioners to attend the funerals of every drowned sailor thrown up on his shore, and some of them plainly black and heathen. There was a little wood near by where he wrote *Trelawny*, a ballad we thundered out at school. At nineteen he married a lady of forty-one and was perfectly happy. And of course he brought harvest parties out of the barn and into the church. Those barn-releases after the incredible toil of reaping by hand have been heavily expurgated. Hardy himself could not describe them. What Robert Hawker did – in 1843 – was to revive the medieval Lammas (loaf-mass) during which bread made from the first corn of the year was consecrated at the altar.

Our harvest festivals are somewhat incoherent attempts to revive an agricultural economy which flourished before combines and supermarkets, post-Spry flower-arranging and the minimalizing of the landworkers. One could truthfully say that there is not an aching back in the nave – at least not from gathering-in. The dark side of the hymns, 'the Angel-reaping o'er', we take in our stride, although I sometimes find myself glancing at a Victorian window to an old couple, the Nottidges, who are being cut down in the field by a bent figure with a sombre halo. Poor Nottidges from the big house opposite, the angel reaping o'er had, long since, gathered their teenage

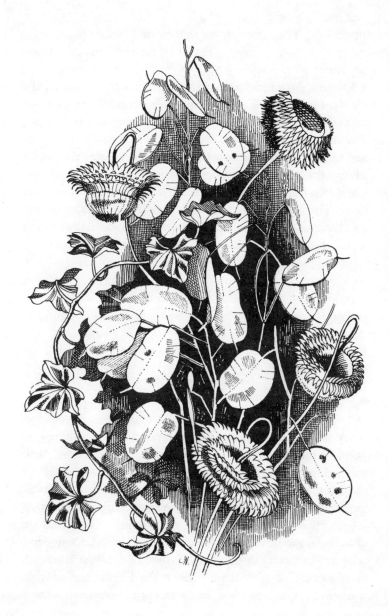

children. To outlive one's children, 'that's not right', as we say in Suffolk. The rightness of things, of festivals particularly, cannot be taken as said; it has to be retaught. Farmer Amos, an earthy young man (and a marvellous poet), denounced religious feasts which left the people spiritually hungry. Beautiful children bring up tokens of today's plenty, tinned soup, baskets of carrots, sweetcorn, Cox's apples – and an oak tree in a pot. Has a potted oak been stood on an altar before – I mean since the Druids? I describe how the farmers on their Sunday walks always took pockets of acorns during October and pressed them into the moist hedgerow soil. 'Where shall we plant your oak?' The little boy is at a loss, half smiles, says nothing. His gift is out of his hands. Back home, plenty in the shape of pears thuds into the long grass.

Michaelmas

Written, appropriately, in the air on the feast of St Michael as the Dallas plane heads home. 'I won't be here next week,' I told the village, 'because I have to go to Texas.' Well, one is born every minute – all that way just to give a talk! And, 'that means you will miss the Mount Bures Harvest Festival?' Some shaking of heads at my flightiness. It came into my mind as we sped through Dallas. It was 90-plus and beyond the air-conditioned car all was a furnace. The baked, tawny land-scape shimmered in the heat all the way to Waco and the university. This is big Baptist country and it was entirely right that my first conversation with a stranger should be one with the Christian name of Jordan. Jordan believed that Waco was about the size of Paris, and that its chief industries included a huge contact-lens manufactory and a vast works which recycled bottle-glass. It was the university's amazing use of glass of another kind which convinced me that here in this old frontier city I was to meet a response to poetry unlike that in any other part of the world. For in the 1950s, under cover of describing it as a library, they built a temple to Robert Browning. This is where over fifty stained glass windows filled with Pippa, the Pied Piper, the Last Duchess, and Joris and Dirck, of course, create a great blue and green lantern into which I stepped from the blaze of noon to enter the sumptuous Victorian imagination.

Outside, an elegance of grackles, if I am allowed to coin a collective noun, held court in the oaks. I admired these pretty birds from Mexico, but nobody else does. Why? 'Because they are too many.' Ah ... Dr Brooks, high priest to the temple of Browning, showed me its treasures as we strolled from mezzanine to mezzanine.

I was publicly prayed for at the official banquet which followed my 'talk' – the annual Beall–Russell Lecture, no less – and the intimacy of it, and the bowed heads over the plates, was disturbing, although in a sweet way. Texas is a good state for discovering what the religious American is. My subject was the poetry of the two world wars and I began by telling the sea of young faces about my father, the country boy at Gallipoli. The old familiar war poetry was quite new here. Beyond the campus flowed the Brazos – the 'arms of God' – and I thought of the settlers and the Indians alike seeking its protection. Where the sun hit it, it became molten brass. I hardly knew where I was, here amidst so much Midwest courtesy, at the Dardanelles with father, or back at Wormingford where I should be with so much fruit to pick. I must see the country they insisted, and so we fled Browning, the classrooms, even the fiery sun, for China Spring and its shade. No grackles. Instead a long-eared owl out-staring us.

Trinity Eighteen

Gathering – one of those ample words which accommodates a whole range of meaning from beneficent collecting-up to ruthless taking. All this because I have been gathering the plums, tugging the laden branches towards me with a rake and stripping from the firm purple-yellow fruits one at a time. The cat has slept in a mouse-brown bed of hay under the plum tree for the past fortnight, watching the stars through its leaves and just using the house as a restaurant. I have gathered the nuts, the blackberries, the tomatoes, the huge prickly seedheads of the artichokes with their silvery bracts, and the runner beans. The apples say, 'us next'. The mechanical hedger, known to Grandfather Brown the farmer as 'the murderer', has done its grim duty and left the lane-sides nice and tidy.

Hebrew law forbade total gathering in the fields and orchards. Something had to be left in the corners for the poor to pick up. Friends arrive for the late-summer loot, knowing just where it lies. Some make for the bay tree, of which it hardly seems grateful to remark that it spreads itself in great power like the wicked. But it is certainly taking over. The cadences of the season are those of Tyndale. His immortal language hangs in the sharp air. I have been hearing what the scholars have been saying about him as his half-millennium approaches, William

Tyndale the gentleman-scholar from a Gloucestershire village who remains more influential than any other English writer, Shakespeare included. At first there was a demented rushing around to gather and incinerate every telling sentence. Imagine attempting to burn out 'In the beginning was the Word . . .' Most of the Authorized Version was essentially Tyndale's version. They strangled and burnt him at Vilvorde. He was aged about forty-two. He came to mind again as I gathered falls, rock-hard Warden pears once thought, when baked, suitable pudding for the higher clergy, and the first-down apples. How did an apple get into the Fall? Tyndale says nothing about an apple, just the 'fruit of the tree' which was 'to be desired to make one wise'. Yet the carol-singers will soon insist that it was 'all for an appil'. How did an apple get into the Fall? Because in St Jerome's Latin Genesis *malum* is the word for both apple and evil.

I have been to visit a sad husband whose wife has been gathered. The emptiness of the small house opposite the cropped field. He takes a paper from behind the clock, the traditional place for letters and instructions, reminders and lists. 'This is what she wanted.' They are the hymns for her funeral, written just three days before. The words tumble about. We have tea. It is the first day of his inadequacy.

Michael Takes Charge

A new priest in charge, at last, at last. We cram into Mount Bures parish church to hear for the first time the voice with which the little benefice will be identified. It is a historic moment. Grand processions squeeze through the crush, hymns are sung where they may be sung, old formularies are affirmed and allegiances sworn, presentations are made, Bishop John blesses Priest Michael, there is clapping of hands and shaking of hands after the handing of him into his stall. Then out into the black night to drive three miles to Wormingford village hall for the party. Two-thirds of the cars make it but then the level crossing gates bar the rest of us from following and I can see the gate-keeper relishing his power. It is not every evening one can hold up half the diocese. These long interregnums, once thought deprivations and spaces, are now recognized as a positive and necessary part of church life, but there is a feeling of rightness and gladness in having an occupied vicarage once more.

Nature's welcome is violent and stentorian. Pent-up skies break into wild thunderstorms which drown the lanes and terrify the beasts, bring down the fruit and wash away any lingering evidence of the heatwave. I hear what sounds like Cornish seas and dash out to find that it is my usually tinkling waterfall belting out gallons per second. Max sits in the window, his unflinching yellow eyes filled with lightning. But the horses gallop across the hillside, full of fear. Hurrying to prevent a shed door being smashed by the 'tempest', as an old man still describes it, I am rained on by acorns as well as showers and I am reminded of the ancient 'right of pannage' which allowed poor men to run their pigs in woodland so that they could feed on acorns and beechmast. An old friend, the son of a Suffolk

farmer, did what generations of his ancestors always made a point of doing at this time of the year, filled his pockets with acorns so that during his autumn walks he could sow them along the hedgerows. Most of the great farm oaks of England were planted like this. I have a round dozen, about a century old, and unusually tall due to having to grow out from a valley and to having their feet in a brook.

Returning from an early morning inspection of the damage – none, as it happened – I hear an exceptional 'Prayer for

Today'. A woman Reader philosophizes on regret – on the years that the locusts have eaten. Henry James did not regret the excesses of his youth, only the 'possibilities I didn't embrace' in 'my chilled age'.

St Francis of Assisi

The distinctive pleasure of being interrupted. Friends arrive with maps where maps are not required. 'Show us where you used to live.' Very well. Off we go via the back road. It is not far to the other life – an hour's drive, maybe. It soon begins to show itself through thinning trees. And there behind the trim hedge lurks another old house in which books were written and silences felt. I stare at the familiar orange pantiles and the hulking Suffolk presence of the building with deep recognition. And then we drive on through the pale day, crunching over beechmast, slowly so as not to miss a thing. At Hoo, that blessed spot on my personal atlas, the October wind gears itself up for a proper blow. We pass the cottage where the ancient woman lived who would see me out with a sharp, 'Come again – but not too soon!' Something grand yet faint, like a town made of clouds, now occupies the horizon – Framlingham. My stream of information divides. My friends hear all about Bloody Mary hurrying from Framlingham Castle to depose Lady Jane Grey, whilst I am telling myself that I am back once again in the land of the three canons. These were rumbustious Bulstrode, gentle Ellis-Jones and learned Gilchrist. Bulstrode was rector of Framlingham and Saxstead where every Wednesday he and his wife would take up residence in a caravan named 'Rectory'; Ellis-Jones was vicar of Charsfield, Hoo and Monewden, and Gilchrist was rector of Dennington where he housed a vast collection of sick-communion cups. All three dear old men are now with God. I see their shadows in the lanes.

Lunch at Framlingham, but in such slow motion that we begin to imagine that we have slipped into one of those time-sequences which even Stephen Hawking is beginning to allow. It could be 1935. The clocks having certainly just been put back, there is a sense of lateness in whatever we do. On to Dennington, for me another special destination, although where, unlike at Hoo which demands the inner eye, there are many astonishing things to see, to touch. For here we are in Chaucer's ancestral fields. The Chaucer family's upward mobility was breathtaking, from Suffolk peasants to a consort's throne via the wine trade, diplomacy and poetry. We enter St Mary's, where they entered in muddy shoes, and which is one of those parish churches to which furnishings are added but nothing is thrown out. I take my friends to the sand-table where the labourers' children learnt their letters and write my name with my finger, then obliterate it. Kate then writes 'Kate' and smooths it out. Peter-Paul writes something then draws the little shutter across it before I can read his sand-language. I recall the Lord writing – what? – with his finger in the dust on the Temple floor. If only one knew. Twice he bent down to write in dust. What was written would have soon been trodden out; the place was always so crowded. All around us soars a forest of spectacular medieval carpentry, fretted rood-screen galleries – even the pyx canopy. Up in the south aisle lies Lord Bardolph, who died in 1441, and who as a boy I wanted to be Nym and Pistol's old mate, but alas not. Horse-chestnut leaves sail down behind the fragmented glass. It is time to go. We have seen enough for one day.

Trinity Nineteen: Harvest Festival

How unjust that a good place should, perhaps for ever, be tagged with a horror visited upon it by a crazed intruder. So I meditated as I flew back from innocent Waco into innocent Cheiry. The bottom-line sanity of what we believe has always entranced me – drawn me into the beauties and satisfactions of Christianity. A strongly held religious daftness does not meet St Paul's famous admittance of being a fool for Christ's sake at any point. But what to do, with millenarianism running mad? Somebody said that the words *'Theodidacta, profunda, ecstatica'* – taught of God, profound, ecstatic – should have been carved on the tomb of Julian of Norwich, and we in the final decade of the twentieth century could do with a lot more spiritual education and depth to go with our often mindless ecstasies. Let the agnostic Larkin's reminder 'A serious house on serious earth it is' be fixed to the south door.

It is Trinity Nineteen and leaves cover the top meadows and the churchyard path, lime-tree leaves, early oak leaves which can't wait for desuetude, and the poplar leaves which used to softly clap in the kitchen garden, but which now sink blackly into the dank grass. The Epistle is apposite to events, with St Paul warning the Ephesus church not to have its 'understanding darkened', not to allow itself to become 'alienated from the life of God through ignorance', not to become 'past feeling'.

At harvest festival the village children troop towards me, half-obscured by their good gifts. A small boy carries a pumpkin so big that it turns him into Atlas bearing up the world. There are baskets of brown eggs, green grapes, russet apples, and tins of this and that to prove that we are aware of Tesco's part in the annual drama of Providence. They glow on the altar like a divine version of the farm-shop counter. The church is full and sweet-smelling, but with an underlying pungency which says October. My address is about Jethro Tull inventing the seed-drill, inspired by the retraction mechanism of the church organ, and putting paid to 'we plough the fields and *scatter*'. Though not for ages because Grandfather Brown, now seated in farmers' pew at the back, scattered seed-corn in his youth skilfully and even-handedly to right and left of him, though with the inevitable wastefulness of the parable. This agricultural lesson over, and the 'holy, aweful Reaper' waiting in the last verse of the last hymn, we emerge to a hint of frost. Lapwings tumble over the ribbed soil, calling with sad voices.

Plenty

Delectable days. St Luke's little summer approaches. Mornings at seven are wreathed in soaking mist and enormous webs supply a kind of white darkness. Mornings at ten are ablaze. The village struggles with 'plenty', or the opposite of enough. Neighbours say that they have never seen anything like it – although they have, of course – but such amazement does at least make us take stock of orchards running over and weather which is bliss beyond compare. After breakfast I hustle through desk-work so as to get out and make the best of it. After supper a story-book moon hangs in the skeiny ultramarine sky as bell practice subsides and the ringers make their way to the Crown. 'More tomorrow!' they promise, meaning not peals but days like this.

I take the last of the harvest festivals, omitting the thanksgiving for Plenty but taking care to include the General Thanksgiving because Phillida loves it. Worshippers have their special devotions. Edward Reynolds wrote it in 1661, the year they made him Bishop of Norwich. His language – 'We bless thee for our creation, preservation, and all the blessings of this life' – and now spoken by us just once a year, excite a quiet but noticeable fervour. They rumble forth. The truth is, this year's plenty is giving us a bit of a headache. What do you give the postman when his van is already bursting with Bramleys? There are plastic bags full of falls at gates saying, 'Take me'. And yet in the supermarkets Golden Delicious, a misnomer if ever there was one, can only be had at a price.

As children we inhabited a universe of gathered or fallen fruit, of jams and kilner-jars, of cookers and eaters, of apples laid out in the larder like regiments, and of waste and rot in the long wet grass. There were days when an apple would be a welcome gift, and days when you let it lie. Vans would take the falls to Debenham to be squeezed into cider. The prodigiousness of nature and the measured-ness of nature, by turn, used to be a yearly hazard. The cry went up, 'They won't keep!' Keep me as the apple of the eye. Meanwhile, fat birds sing opportunely in the groaning hedges and I see that even the rhubarb is having a final flourish. But the deep-freeze implores 'No more!' We must certainly keep our heads. Sensible Bishop Reynolds tells us to ask God to 'give us that due sense of all thy mercies, that our hearts may be unfeignedly thankful . . .'

One of his mercies, or October miracles, is that my fairy-ring champignon have survived the mower. They bloom, if that is the word, in their circle, concentric, untouched, as they have done since my boyhood.

Trinity Twenty: St Luke

'Are you haunted?' the fine-weather visitors enquire. 'You can tell us about the local ghosts,' says the young man who is making a Hallowe'en programme for Ipswich Radio. To the visitors I give an untruthful no, not wishing to explain the not ghostly encounters one has in any ancient house; to Ipswich Radio I give the famous story of Black Shuck, a calf-sized dog who terrorized Suffolk church-goers long ago, a supernatural beast against which the hound of the Baskervilles was no more than a playful puppy. Many a poor soul praying 'by thy great mercy defend us from all perils and dangers of this night' was thinking of Shuck. My neighbour William, ninety-six last Michaelmas, brought the haunting question up as we watched a freshly drilled wheatfield in peerless October sunshine. He said, 'I dare say that you will have heard of the *presence* in our sitting-room . . .' That's it, I told myself, not a ghost but a presence, or, as the dictionary puts it, 'an incorporeal being or influence felt or conceived as present'. I had indeed heard of his presence. It is that of a dairy-farmer's wife who appears to have left a wake of busyness behind her. 'We are sitting by the fire and she hurries past.' Our talk drifts to the tithe-war of the 1920s, when the poverty-stricken farmers mutinied against a medieval tax which the Church of England still demanded. Ghostly reminiscences of the tithe-war rallies come back to me. William and I sit in his car which is parked by the great field where the wheat is so new and what we remember is so old. Wherever we look there is a presence.

Part of my busyness this week is concerned with the annual service for the Essex Association of Change Ringers. St Luke's little summer goes on and on in every variation of goldenness, the yellow hazel leaves lying on the graves like ancient coins, and ash leaves sailing past my window like withered hands. On this still afternoon, the feast of that intensely active woman St Teresa of Avila, along they come, the tower captains and rookies, the bell-masters and bell-learners, those who have rung for a lifetime and those who will, to set the Little Horkesley ring through its paces. I too have to ring the changes in the sermon, having taken so many of these bell-evensongs, and so I preach on 'Who listens?' Meriel plays a bell-hymn with its 'Great the God-fearing with each iron tongue', and there is tea and speeches. Then more hours of bell-music. 'You were going it last night!' said somebody the next morning. 'You'll be waking the dead!'

The winds strengthen, the leaves fall in hosts yet so individually. The fruit trees are stripped but in the woodland there is a bearing-up of foliage until the moment arrives when each leaf lets go, itself to the end. Miss Beaumont was like this, letting go just before her ninetieth birthday. Who will reprimand us now? She was our heroine – we can say it now that she is out of hearing. Images of her conflict. There is Sister Beau of the Burma Road and there is the formidable old woman making her precarious journey to the altar-rail in the church where she was baptized at Easter 1905, every step of the way milkily indistinct, every line of the singing far off, as in another place. She did not suffer fools or indeed anything gladly. She had nursed from the East End to the Chindwin River and was the enemy of all suffering, physical or otherwise. Her family had kept our pub and on troopships and by battlegrounds the other nurses would say, 'Tell us about your village, Beau.' So she did until, when we all knew her, she had become a riotous raconteuse. Travelling to a distant funeral with her, I wondered whether I would have the strength to get out of the car, the laughter shaking every mile. But in the little Roman Catholic church, hanging on to my arm, bumping into things, her large body collapsed into sorrow for the dead.

Her nieces brought me her commands for her funeral and I passed them on to the parish. Instant obedience. One, the bells are to peal, not toll. Two, we are to wear button-holes and bring late flowers from our gardens and ourselves carry them to her grave, and not to give them to the undertaker. Three, we are to sing 'The Lord of the Dance', 'Jesus Christ is Risen Today' and Psalm 150. Four, her grave is to be grassed over and no stone erected. Five, if we must, we can buy something sensible for Wormingford in her memory. Six (unwritten) we are not to do ridiculous things just because she isn't here to lay down the law. This law of Miss Beaumont's was an astringent version of Christ's law, stinging and inescapable like iodine.

She carried little with her through an enormously hard-working life. In Burma she found 'a piece of tin' bearing the words 'Lest we forget' pricked out in holes made by a nail and the heel of a boot. A soldier's tribute to a dead comrade. 'Like a bad conscience, it lies at the bottom of my trunk, reminding me of a promise made and never kept.' Number seven – at the funeral – I am ordered to read from the pulpit this promise made and never kept. I do so wearing a Gloire de Dijon rose on my stole.

Trinity Twenty-one: in Australia

We drive to Sydney in the brilliant October sun for choral Eucharist at St James's Church on 'the Twenty-ninth Sunday in Ordinary Time'. Botany Bay sparkles and surfers speed past us in the opposite direction. The church is elegant Georgian, designed by a convict architect and built by convict labour. It might be in Cheltenham. There is an expectant congregation and Bishop Anthony from the Outback to preach. I am taken aback by the grandeur of the service, which could be worth the price of an air ticket for a connoisseur of Anglican liturgy. A long white river of choir, each singer one yard precisely from the next, a mighty organ and Pitoni's *Cantate Domino* as introit. No dreaming off into prayer here: I must concentrate. A pair of women deacons sweep down the aisle bearing aloft what looks like the Book of Kells. The drilled beauty of music, language and gesture is loaded with historic references, but you need your wits about you.

The sermon is learned and toughly delivered by the lean brown bishop who paints a harsh picture of his burnt-up diocese. Archbishop Tutu preaches next door, another realist. Parched goldfields, failing agriculture, the new South Africa and our text from Psalm 96 – 'Ascribe to the Lord the honour due to name ... He will judge the world with righteousness, and the peoples with his truth.' This celebration during Ordinary Time takes nearly two hours. We return to lunch via the University, where students eat fast food on the hot grass. I think of the poor felons baking bricks for St James's and pining for Gloucester or Wapping. Or possibly Wormingford.

Spring in New South Wales. Acres of bluebells at Everglades in the Blue Mountains. I wake early in the now familiar room overlooking Gymea Bay and remember the suddenness of spring flowers. My bed is in my brother's library and here and there, easily at hand, are objects from our childhood in Suffolk. The Bay is named after the ten-foot lilies which glow in the bush at this time of the year. Dropping to it in a series of steep lawns and walls is my brother's Eden, the garden which he has been creating for upward of thirty years. Guarding the door is the huge brass-rubbing of Sir Robert de Bures, 1302, from the church where our parents were married, and we were baptized. It is one of the oldest and best brasses in Britain and I can remember rubbing it with heel-ball and kitchen paper. This image is all bright gold as though our old hero has polished himself up so as not to let us down in a Southern hemisphere. He and his lion had lain in our chancel for half a millennium before Captain Cook weighed anchor at Kernell, a point just out of sight from my window. This is the lovely, tragic land of the first settlers, their original shire, Sutherland. It is named after Seaman Sutherland, a sailor from Orkney, who died from TB before he could step ashore. They buried him in the Kernell sand. No burnished brass for him, instead, his name flashes in neon a thousand times along the motorways.

About five p.m. a half-hearted dawn chorus of raucous screams and mellifluous chimes disturbs the absolute silence of prehistory. Birds of unlikely proportions, noisiness and hue, rosannas, galahs, cockatoos and kookaburras, are stirring. Here the magpie is melodious. Here in mid-spring they feed on mulberries.

Trinity Twenty-two: in Australia

My brother takes me to Canberra on the plane to show me Australia's inconvenient capital, and to lunch with his friend Mr Dobie of the House of Representatives. The air is what the old travel writers used to call pellucid. The enormous Parliament House hides in a hill, as if to shield its extravagance from the ratepayers. One enters through a forest of polished grey marble columns which are designed to suggest a eucalyptus grove and eventually, after a long journey through courts and interior gardens, arrives on the roof, which is a lawn from which one can stroll down to the street. Breast-shaped hills from which the city takes its Aboriginal name surround it in a circle. I can see the War Memorial, where the Unknown Warrior is to be buried this Remembrance Sunday. So lengthy and startling is this afterthought that it seems to have left most Australians speechless.

After lunch I am taken to the Visitors' Gallery to hear a roaring debate on Aborigine land rights and to watch the Prime Minister Mr Keating sweep out in high dudgeon, or maybe because he couldn't get a word in. It is Westminster all over again – except for the members' offices, which are palatial. I think of our new MPs desperately searching around for a gothic window-sill for their secretaries to perch on. Both here in Canberra and wherever I go I listen to pro- and anti-mutterings re Mr Keating's dream of a republic. The Queen's witty response is not what was expected from her and there is some scratching of heads. Have they a prospective president in mind? Blank faces. It need not be a politician. Relieved faces. We stroll to the creamy Empire buildings of George V's Canberra and see him reigning from his plinth. There is hardly a soul about, here, in the High Court, in the National Gallery, in the rolling parks, anywhere. Canberra is a capital waiting a population, waiting to have its pristine glories smudged a little by human breath and feet. Yet stone-age breath and feet both here and by the river at Wormingford.

Trinity Twenty-three: still in Australia

To Homebush, where they are constructing the centre for the Olympic Games. A kind rock-blaster guides us around. Australia's manageable surface is only skin deep, as it were. The spade soon hits the sandstone. You can't put up a shed without calling in the rock-blaster. Homebush, the site of the AD 2000 Games was a vast abattoir, an enormous shambles, a field of slaughter for Sydney. But now – and already – what a transformation! There is nothing comparable in Britain to the way in which Australia, and some parts of the United States, gets on with things. Stadia, housing, swimming-pools, hotels, gardens, all the architectural optimism, all the clan of white walls and whipping national flags seemed to be rising by the minute. Made to wear a tin helmet and uncrushable boots like a visiting VIP, I murmur, 'But you have seven more years . . .' I am actually sitting where everything is so ready that all one needs is the starting gun. Nobody is sorry for Manchester. They have planted 100 year-old trees and they stand in a cat's cradle of guy ropes. Homebush is no place for saplings. All over the globe athletes are limbering up. Homebush, place of blood, your better days have come.

*

To Wollongong, but first to Bulli, where arum lilies grow wild and in such rough profusion as to break their association with brides and altars. Vast red cliffs lurch over the Tasman Sea. There are ways of getting up and down them via ancient tracks, yet the most untrodden wastes of Britain are cosy in comparison. The little house by the shore where D. H. Lawrence wrote *Kangaroo* is not far off. He was seething with indignation at what had happened to him and Frieda in Cornwall and had fled that granite for these dizzy rocks. European Australia knows its origins down to the day and hour but Aboriginal Australia is year-less. Every day, for a month, I am a traveller in both of these territories, constantly adjusting my gaze and correcting my perspective. But, 'Walk on!' – the Buddha's last word to his followers. 'Walk worthy of God,' Paul told the Thessalonians.

Tonight, *Don Giovanni* in the shell-topped Opera House and with Stephen Bennett looking about as capable of the deeds he is singing as the night birds soaring towards Manley.

I am reading Kierkegaard. Let loose among my brother's books after a strenuous day in the rainforest, I discover the marvellous *Journals* which Kierkegaard wrote between 1846 and 1855, and am ravished. Such writing wants me to tell the Church, 'Plant nothing fresh by way of progress and change until you have taken another look at what has been set aside.' As I turn the pages I think yet again of that timeless reading-list I would like to draw up for convert and ordinand alike, and of what hay I would like to make of some of the offerings in the Christian Bookshop.

Søren Kierkegaard:

It is very dangerous to go into eternity with possibilities which one has oneself prevented from becoming realities. A possibility is a hint from God. One must follow it. In every man there is latent the highest possibility; one must follow it. If God does not wish it, then let him prevent it, but one must not hinder oneself. A priest or layman who hinders his own highest possibility hinders that of his parish.

There should be a hymn 'O worship the Lord in the beauty of seriousness.'

I do a little songlining à la Bruce Chatwyn, whose travels in Aboriginal Australia are so eloquently described that they would tempt anyone to step straight out of the manicured Sydney suburbs into the adjacent wilds. 'I have a vision of the Songlines stretching across the continents and ages; that wherever men have trodden they have left a trail of song . . . where the First Man shouted the opening stanza of the World Song, "I am!".' Adam singing. Eve too, of course. My nephew takes me to a Dreaming place on the heights above Port Jackson. It is a rock plateau covered with carvings which in Europe would have been made during the Stone Age but here at any time up to the near present. There are animals and human beings, and one of the rocks has been shallowly scooped out to make a basin. The beach below is strewn with lovers, and sailing-ships gleam on the horizon. I think of the ferocious accounts of the Aborigines in the Reverend Richard Cobbold's *Margaret Catchpole*, a melodramatic novel which established this lady horse-thief as Suffolk's folk-heroine. How we thrilled to it as boys. But no opening stanza of the World Song there, only a Victorian clergyman's nervous view of the savage. *The Songlines* is a soliloquy on walking, on the Way, the Path. I trust lots of Sydney-dwellers will read it, for I have never seen such a car-bound society. The early Christians walked in imitation of the Lord.

All Saints

Heavy beating rain on the window and from the long ago a voice saying the obvious – 'No, you can't go out!' My imprisoned face against the pane. Now what shall I do? What will the farmworkers do as they splosh off the sodden fields and won't be paid? There was never enough wages for some to be put by for a rainy day. This is what the old saying meant. A drowning All Saints' rain thrashes the trees and scrubs the flints and then, when it feels that it can do no more, it turns itself off and I can leave the house. But don't go far, warns the sky. It is mild as well as wet and the house tops steam. Wet-through ramblers pause to consult their soaked map. They have shining faces and clay feet. They raise their faces to the fast-approaching 'next lot' and are happy.

In the vestry I check the list of the departed, adding my parents' names and those of some friends. Every now and then on this All Souls' register the name of a 'dormitory' villager appears, the name of someone who never shared in our parochiality yet will for ever be part of the parish dust – usually via the crematorium. This being able to live anonymously and disconnected in an English village is a phenomenon of our day. It could never have happened in my childhood, when the entire population would have joined nosy forces to investigate anyone who so much as attempted it. But now nobody minds whether the incomers join in or not. Social historians are rather indignant at such detachment. I know at least a dozen residents about whom I know nothing. When we pass each other's houses we shout, 'Nice weather for ducks!' – or something equally uninquisitive. But when they die they enter our churchyard by right and sleep alongside the most indigenous of us.

I have always liked the masterly juxtaposition of the Epistle and Gospel for All Saints, and the Collect's leading us via the blessed ones to 'unspeakable joys' is breathtaking. The Epistle is John's vision of multitudinous saints drawn from every part of the world, and the Gospel is the Lord's telling the Twelve about the nine states of blessedness. Rain-beads chase each other down the painted glass as we sing, Holy, holy, holy. We pick our way between pools to cars. The rookery is dark with drenched birds.

All Souls

Hard frosts at last. They caught the roses which had been playing a kind of horticultural 'last across'. Caught the village too, sharply reminding it that it was not in Provence. Friends arrive to help me dig out the water-course. For a few seconds the spade acts as a suture, cutting off the flow. Then the spring – springs! We rake the dark humus from its swift path to the house, to the pond, to the river. Max brings us a mouse, then swallows it before our eyes. Muddy but triumphant, we sit on the bank and eat elevenses. It is November and as far from Tom Hood's murky poem – 'No sun – no moon!/ No morn – no noon . . . No fruits, no flowers, no leaves, no birds' – as it is possible to be. A revisionary verse is needed: 'No fog, no smog', etc. I enquire of Joachim, who has arrived from Berlin, although not specifically to help me clean out my ditch, what it is like there. 'Dank not bright, cooling, quiet'. Middle Europe tasting its winter.

The names of the departed are read on All Saints and All

Souls. Michael comes to 'for all thy servants departed this life in thy faith and fear' and I speak the names of the dead. It is like the school register, but what a big class! I see their owners in their old places and, by the time I reach the end of the list, packing the church. Some of us occupying dead men's pews feel apologetic. Widows and widowers crouch in an enormous silence. The communion of saints moves on. There are stricken trees in the churchyard, killed not by frost but by drought, a twisted cherry and a parasol-shaped hawthorn, both decorative in their senescence. We hurry home.

To Mount Bures the following Sunday to talk about Paul's letter to Philemon. Whenever I come to this little church on its spur above the Colne valley the apocryphal words of St John in his old age return to me – 'It will suffice.' He was pestered for details about the Lord ('And did you once see Jesus plain?') but all he would say was, 'Little children, love one another.' 'Is that all?' 'It will suffice.' Often in remote country churches like Mount Bures in which a dozen worshippers sing and pray as best they can, I tell myself, 'It will suffice.' The vast historic superstructure of Christianity in all its forms steps aside to allow the validity of our simple matins. Philemon, the lesson, is Paul's only private letter to have survived and it is 'just a few lines' about Onesimus the runaway slave. Onesimus means profitable. Paul, from prison, destroys the then natural order of his friend Philemon's housekeeping by returning his runaway slave with a note saying, 'Here is your brother and my son.' No wonder Nero destroyed the first Christians. Set slaves free, and where would you be! Fortunately for profits, centuries of later Christians ignored Paul's letter to Philemon.

St Leonard

The golden autumn falters on and it is hard to stay indoors. An arrested stillness alternates with a warm blustery wind. Kate telephones to remind me that the theme for the monthly family service at Little Horkesley is Moses in the Bulrushes. The founder of Israel is in hiding among the papyrus of Egypt. There's a thought – except that it is far too grown-up for the angelic host filling the aisle. And so, of course, is the reason for Moses being where he was. Artful midwives, genocide, ethnic cleansing, secret fostering, and all the horrible Herod stuff in an earlier version. So I extract a perfectly truthful tale about a clever princess and a brave mother, putting in a good word for fathers, quite a few of these being present. Now and then I look over my glasses and ask the surprise question, which one is supposed to do on these occasions. A volley of answers. Being themselves river-bank children, the angelic host is great on bulrushes. I shift child-welfare on to such matters as cygnet-welfare, robin-welfare, kitten-welfare and, eventually, to the welfare of the boy Jesus. We are now well away from the hideously adult happenings by the Nile all those centuries ago. Sweet singing follows. Two seraphs bring up the offertory, slapping it down on the dish. There is lemonade at the back of the church, there are conkers in the churchyard, there will be a rush home for the real eating. I hardly know their names and never glimpse them except at this service.

Walking back I pass Lower Bottoms, the hilly meadow on the left of the lane through which springs and rivulets tinkle all year long, and recall a Victorian photograph. It is of a group of basket-makers seated on the grass in this very spot. There are piles of osiers and rushes, and also a heap of lovely new baskets, each one as fresh as a daisy. There are frails for seed-corn, apple-skips, washing-baskets, shopping-baskets for market-day in Colchester, bait (farmworkers' lunch) baskets and fish-baskets. There are, too, Moses-baskets made of soft yellow straw which would be filled, first with a layette, then with a new baby. Plastic has routed willow, straw and rushes. But there are still plenty of bulrushes in the Stour, although the river-reeve at Bures no longer sees them as a crop, and the river itself is less concealed than it was. A kestrel hangs stationary above where the old basket-makers wove in and out. In their day such busy places would be full of children running loose. It is St Leonard's day – my birthday. He is the saint of prisoners, of the confined. The village children no longer run through the meadows and are rarely visible. My talk on the royally protected Moses would have made sense to them.

The making redundant of St Leonard's church in nearby Colchester was a sad business, but it brought us at Wormingford much good in the persons of the organist and ringers. However, their hearts remain in that lovely deserted building by the river. On the saint's day they return to it for annual evensong and its windows are lit up above the landing-stage where the Romans victualled their garrison. It was built at the height of his cult but on sinking sand or its equivalent. It buckled, wavered, was shorn-up, still stands, should be reconsidered, used. Generations sang 'Keep me as the apple of the eye' in it.

My crab-apples cannot be kept. They are too many. Thousands of them have rained down on Duncan's field to make a pale yellow carpet full of bumps and hollows. Two or three crabs are said to make all the difference to an apple-pie and just a few dozen are enough for a year's supply of jelly. So what of the myriad rest of them? Let them lie in the harvest's aftermath, let them feed the stubble. Let *Malus sylvestris*, their mother-tree, look down on her yearly avalanche with no feeling of waste, only of plenitude. Crabbed suggests shrivelled but

there is something wonderfully rounded in the lustrous shed-
ding of so many little apples. The mother-tree herself could
scarcely be less crabbed and in May she is a blossoming sight
worth anyone's journey. The wilding-tree, they used to call her.
St Leonard's prisoners in their dungeons must have hungered
for wild creatures and wilding-trees, and the sick folk who
prayed to him for a return of their wild strength.

November is the season of Proverbs. They are to be read
morning and evening. Part of the Book of Proverbs is taken
from a feast of wisdom, part from a feast of folly. Many have
long-entered the language. Others have succeeded in keeping
out of common knowledge so that when they are read out to
us from the lectern, we sit up. The Book says that a wise man
will go out of his way to understand a proverb.

Somewhat daringly, I decide to preach on Wisdom. The old
pulpits and the lower panels of rood-screens used to have wise
faces on them, the portraits of the Fathers. Everyone knows
that I would not have been among them – too fanciful for one
thing. I talk about the Book of Proverbs, the collection of
sayings which taught George Herbert the art of compression,
directness and simplicity. He and his brother Henry themselves
collected a thousand such sayings and called their book *Outland-
ish Proverbs*. Here are two proverbs from it. 'When a friend asks,
there is no tomorrow.' 'Living well is the best revenge.'

Remembrance

A day of peerless melancholy. Drizzle dying out and a pink and brown drift of sky. A wet Union Jack sags over the homely brick finials of the tower and the ringers are at work. The church is full and the grey day does wonders for what colour there is, intensifying it. Cherry-red scraps of old glass and the fierce red of artificial poppies fire the interior. Donald reads the names of the fallen. How 'fallen'? That is for me to say later on. But first there is a recorded trumpeter's Last Post. And so the formal rite begins, with old people seeing what the young will never see, and the old sadness being revived. To rob the service of its clichés, I read the whole of Laurence Binyon's poem from the pulpit, putting the famous words in their context. It was written at the very beginning of the First World War and published in *The Times* in September 1914. Binyon was then in his forties, a librarian at the British Museum, also an expert on English watercolours. He is the poet of November. In *The Burning of the Leaves* he describes how

> A flame seizes the smouldering ruin and bites
> On stubborn stalks that crackle as they resist.

I conclude with what is for me the noblest of all written remembrances, that which begins, 'But the souls of the righteous are in the hands of God and there shall no torment touch them,' and which ends with 'they shall shine, and run to and fro like sparks among the stubble.' Like everyone else present, I am staring through smoky time at some face which only I can recognize.

Immediately afterwards we drive to the American aerodrome. The drizzle has stopped and the Stars and Stripes by the memorial to the Hundred Lieutenants is held out by a drying breeze. Would they have heard of Laurence Binyon, the poet who died the same year they came to England? No. We hear how they shall not grow old, as many of us have done. Soon we shall be in the Crown, where they took the village girls half a century ago, young sparks among the stubble. Cars swish past us on the polished surface of the lane. We are touched, privately moved. Binyon, the reconciler of early death was himself seventy-four when he died.

In Memoriam

A dvent steals up on us and in a day or two the sublime words 'Almighty God, give us grace that we may cast away the works of darkness, and put upon us the armour of light, now in the time of this mortal life . . .' will drift through the autumn church and lodge like leaves in our consciousness. Draw us 'from the dread caverns of the grave', we shall beseech. The days do not so much break as emerge. Milky sun and milky moon share the same obscure sky and the fields and hedgerows cannot see where they are going. 'O come, O come, thou Dayspring bright!' we shall implore, wiping the dag from our glasses. The school bus creeps through the lanes devouring a boy here, a girl there. The rookeries are chaotic. One feels that some authoritative teacher-bird should cry, 'Settle down!' Or take a lesson from those high-flying geese winging in a great V to the mere. In just a month, I tell the congregation, the Creator will be born into his creation. 'Please, what is Adonais?'

a child asks. '*Who*, not what.' 'Who, then?' Cars swish home amidst little calls and invitations.

On Thursday a journey to the Queen's Chapel of the Savoy. As I always find London delightful to walk in, I do the last mile on foot. Smoke-free Novembers do wonders for plane trees and Portland stone. The tourists have decamped and the pavements are free. I have to give the address at Monty's memorial service. He was an old Suffolk friend and neighbour so the Chapel is filled with Suffolk faces. How clever of them to have found their way into this splendour. There is Monty's dear wife. They were married here long ago and this is also her birthday. He was a Spitfire pilot, poet, businessman, occasional organist but not, it has to be said, wholly practical. What he could do he did brilliantly and what he could not do he could never learn to do. He and I had much in common in this respect. He was a man whose twenty-two-year-old smile never wore out even in old age. He lies in the earth of a village whose name, very suitably for Monty, means Hawks' hill. His son reads a poem which Monty wrote to his Spitfire and I tell his tale as best I can, and including the story of what happened when the tower of his parish church crashed into the nave – and on Ascension Day! Faced with such devastation, Monty's practicality amounted to genius. Looking down from the Savoy pulpit, I could see the young airman and his bride, and all the accidents and purposes of history which brought the three of us together. At the end I read W. J. Turner's wartime poem *The Young and the Old*. I thought that it could be slipped into Monty's CV with some relevance and would make him grin. Chaucer was married here – another Suffolk bridegroom.

Trinity Twenty-four

Recollecting, the Vote. The aisles are still upright, the congregation undazed, a Collect apt. 'Lord, we beseech thee to keep thy household the Church in continual godliness.' Golden leaves float by the windows on a soft wind. I preach on Romans 16:1 'I commend to you Phoebe, a fellow-Christian who holds office in the congregation at Cenchreae. Give her, in the fellowship of the Lord, a welcome worthy of God's people, and stand by her in any business in which she may need your help.' These proto-Christian ladies from Paul's letters are old friends of mine. Timothy's grandmother, Julia, Prisca, Claudia, I see their Romano-Greek–Hebrew faces in the rush-light of safe houses. Phoebe lived by the harbour at Corinth, a tough spot, no doubt.

The trouble with a writer's diary is that it is bound to contain many days when 'nothing happens'. Nothing other than writing, that is. Especially now, when the light is failing and the mud is rising, and letters from friends in towns stress the decision 'to see you in the spring'. I am out of bounds. So I write, then have breaks splitting logs. The creamy ash-wood parts under the new axe, reminding me of what we said as boys, 'So perish all traitors!'

Neighbours telephone on such crucial matters as bells, the Government's policy re our grant-aided village school, cancer, planting pollinators. I make notes for the first chapter of my existence, recalling what my now long-dead parents told me about how they bowled down the church avenue in the borrowed vicarage brougham after their wedding, ribbon tied to the door-handles. A full lifetime later I peer through the same straight trees towards the suggestion of a tower in the November dark.

Work done, I make bread from 3½ lbs of Sainsbury's flour

and then discover that tomorrow's second lesson has the Lord likening the kingdom to the yeast 'which a woman took and mixed with *half a hundredweight* of flour'. This puts my loaves in their place.

Rain is due. It is official. I get up at six to scythe the orchard before it arrives. The postman can hardly believe his eyes. I have to cut the orchard at about this moment so that the wild flower seeds can fall back into it. My blade uncovers toads and cowslip rosettes which say mind your big feet. There is stormy weather in the tree-tops but none below. It is coming, the deluge. It will bring down the Harden pears, which are not called this for nothing. Picking up the last windfalls, I am reminded of great-aunt Agnes Bean who would only give us little boys wormy Bramleys found in the rank grass – 'Eat the good side'. Picked apples were for her apple-room where they were called 'keepers'. I observe that a tall hazel sprouts from her grave, pushing the stone awry. 'Whatever next!' she would have said. She lived in ceaseless amazement at the nerve of things. I have noticed in village talk how it is polite to show all the incredulity one can, to accept all news with wonder. It blows wet rather than pours in the evening and is quite suddenly cold, but summer stays trapped in the old rooms, and will do for weeks ahead.

St Edmund, King and Martyr

I see with a start that the great ash by the brook is naked and that the hawthorn is blackening. So it has begun at last, senescence. Frosts and gales will no doubt give their *coup de grâce* to the rose-heads. A single heavy shower makes my wellingtons squelch, a noise I don't seem to have heard for ages. Each afternoon I saw-up seasoned willow for the winter fires. The bark falls off like loosened wrappings to the surprise of the woodlice. I offer Hindu apologies. At night I cover a superb spike of yucca bloom with plastic so that further flowers are not nipped in the bud. Some are saved, some sacrificed in this our mortal life. The week has witnessed the tentative sentences of a new book and a host of tasks from the reminder headed 'To be Done' which hangs by my desk. These include the Christmas services, and all the services in between. Michael and I scribble away in our diaries. When a new priest arrived in my old parish he was greeted with, 'You'm must winter us and summer us, sir.' In the pub it was, 'Where do they say he come from – *Wales*?' Ah well, we have to come from somewhere, they supposed. Barrie has circulated the menu for the annual bellringers' dinner at the Crown and we are to tick turkey or beef. Ever mindful of the needs of the clergy, I remind him – unnecessarily – that the vicar is vegetarian. In a village ninety per cent of parochial advice is superfluous. Everyone knows exactly what to do. 'It's all in hand,' they say. And it is. Fool to think otherwise.

I talk to or at the Writers' Workshop in the town. We are in the old High School for Girls. On this spot a decade or so after the Crucifixion the Emperor Claudius was made a god. As a boy I imagined him bowling along up the High Street in his chariot, past Woolworths, past the George Hotel to the forum, the divine Claudius in our very borough. And at the very moment when St Paul was writing his letters. I don't, of course, mention any of this at the Writers' Workshop. What these mature students want to hear is hard information about getting published. But I cannot give this either – who can these days? So I ramble on autobiographically and words like 'discipline' and 'solitude', 'reading' (great emphasis) and 'imagination' come and go. The many writers' workshops I have said these words to pass before me like the life of a drowning man. A youngster tells me that he intends to give up everything to be a poet, adding the Augustinian rider, 'Though not for a bit as I intend to take a break.' Outside the autumn rain pelts down where the unholy emperor trod, now the car-park. Mature ladies dream of being in paperback.

Second Before Advent

About once a month I do what some of my young neighbours do every day – come home from London on the 5.30. The commuters read for a bit then doze, their faces made strangely pure and calm by the simple closing of the eyes. We hurry along through intermittent light and the blackest darkness. A Chinese man telephones his wife. 'Where are we?' He presses his nose against the window like a child. Who could tell? Soon I am walking the last mile in the seeable night of the countryside, picking my way between the watery ruts, murmuring to the horses clustering under the stars, apologizing to some unidentifiable birds which have fled from a holly in noisy commotion.

Then the house looms ahead as it has done for centuries. It has great presence.

Advent approaches and we are to bestir ourselves, shake off our torpor. Let there be no more suspension of what we are capable. All the same I find myself thinking of Tennyson's lotus-eaters with their 'half-dropt eyelids' and their beds of asphodel, and their sleepy 'Let us alone', as this is a philosophy I frequently share with the cat. I am reminded too of the new Rector of Bemerton who, do what he would, found his villagers 'thick and heavy, and hard to raise to a point of zeal and fervency' and who needed 'a mountain of fire to kindle them'. I am, of course, a notorious lotus-eater in our parish, not having to go to work, 'just sitting there writing', and I admit such a blessing. I must admit to an absence of the thick and heavy and unkindled in our worshipping community. They are good to each other. There is a lot of illness, many difficulties, so much practical love and unmentioned care. The farmworker's wife takes food to the wanderer who sometimes sleeps in the bus-shelter, there is far more than just visiting, there is an alert gaze. What cannot be known are our individual reactions to the immanence of Christ. Our readiness would be vague and incoherent were it not for the hymn-poets; they drive us towards splendour, towards gratefulness – and towards dread. They stir us.

Contrary to what is supposed to happen as the year fades and the oak-leaves fall in bitter shoals, I find myself getting up earlier and earlier in the luxury of not having to. It is then that I am 'awake' in a way which is unlike the normal alertness of the daylit hours.

Sunday Next Before Advent

I had an old friend who spoke of his calling – not his trade – milling. The voice of this neighbour, long dead, continues when there are strong winds. Burke thought it a high calling for Britons to have 'turned a savage wilderness into a glorious empire', which shows how little he knew about wildernesses. The liturgy for Andrew our village protector is all calling. My voice echoes in the late-November nave. He was called, I am called to follow a calling. We sing Mrs Alexander's hymn about being called o'er the tumult, which for most of us present at this moment has to be the Budget, the latest version of her 'vain world's golden store'. I read from Romans that Christ is rich unto all that call upon him.

The ringers have rung Andrew in. Two of the bells are the

work of Joanna Sturdy, a woman founder who took over her husband's calling when he died. The village is said to possess very strange acoustics so that its bell music tumbles into various hollows and pockets, or floats down the river. The ringers cite far worse oddities. Liverpool Cathedral, for instance, 'the bells so high that you can't hear them unless you are in Birkenhead!' For our ringers the 'Any Other Business' on the PCC agenda means bell business. This week it is muffles, which 'are only £12 each'. Did we know that they had to *borrow* muffles, and them half worn-out? We sanction muffles. There will be relieved faces at the annual Bellringers' Dinner at the Crown this Friday, where the guest of honour is the Vice-Chancellor of Essex University, a splendid ringer and clever enough to have written a book on the subject. The Bible is bell-less, unless one includes the gold bells which, alternating with blue pomegranates, tinkled along the hem of Aaron's robe. A curious fact, Aaron had the words 'Holiness to the Lord' written on his head-dress; Zechariah sees them engraved on horse-bells.

December has come with almost my favourite weather, which is a kind of warm, muted lemon and grey calmness, with the sun rolling up from behind Duncan's white barn with no intention of doing anything more than a little gilding here and there. Landscape so touched is exquisite. Were I imperializing somebody's 'wilderness' long ago, this is what I would be homesick for, a still December day. Its shine dimmed by cloud cover, its benignity felt.

Tramping to the top to fetch the milk, I find myself thinking of William Temple – perhaps because during times of uproar all previous ages have a way of appearing becalmed in the best kind of orthodoxy. Old friends with scant history assure me this was so. 'Why do they have to change everything?' The history of the Church is partly a history of the re-creation of tradition. Temple had just two and a half years – the same as

George Herbert – in which to play his re-creational role. Neither knew that they had changed everything. Temple was originally refused ordination because of being 'unsafe'.

To St Edmund's Church at East Mersea on St Edmund's day to preach at the patronal festival. Malcolm Oliver the master bellringer drives me across the Strood to the dark flat island. The church is elegant and airy and gently lit by oil lamps. Its single Richard the Secondish bell clangs out over the black fields for the Elevation. My address might have been called 'Will the real Edmund stand up' as I extricate the man from the myths. But it is not the saint who looms over me in this intensely evocative place, but Sabine Baring-Gould, its formidable rector during the 1870s. I hear him rehearsing his fishermen-farming-a-bit-on-the-side-smuggling parishioners in 'Now the Day is Over'. Tall John Swallow now occupies his seat. The church is full, faces indistinct and time 'thrown-out' by persistent notions of eternity. We get home dreadfully late for Malcolm, who has to help drive the first commuter train from Colchester to London in the morning.

The Everlasting Circle

The sacred year ends with a fisherman and begins with a craftsman. Andrew and Eloi the metalworker meet at midnight on the last day of November, and the seasons repeat their rounds. In the village there is a blurring of the old distinctions due to there being perhaps no more than a score of its inhabitants still on the land and to changes in the weather not getting into the houses to any dominant extent. There has to be a heavy snow or a heavy blow for us to say things like, 'It got right into the house!' Until double-glazing etc., weather had every intention of breaking and entering, and if you lived in the country it was November inside and out. All the same, November in the valley was always more late summer than early winter, though tinged with loss and decay. Its last Gospel is about that impromptu picnic when five loaves and two fish, distributed to the Twelve by Christ, and by them to multitudinous mankind, proved to be more than enough to satisfy its hunger.

It gets harder and harder in rural life to keep liturgy and everyday experience in meaningful rotation, to keep worship out of the theme park, to get a chilly wisp of November into the church. Out of the all-the-year heatwave of the car and into a vast old room which, in spite of switching on, at enormous expense, every bar an hour before the service, strikes, if not exactly cold, well, as though the days are pulling in. The congregation is annually puzzled by the everlasting circle and can never make out why it should run from Eloi to Andrew, and not from New Year to Old Year.

I walk in the woods. They are perfectly liturgical. By late November their leaves are down and they are structurally naked and soaring. Homing creatures scuttle about. I wade through this year's leaves, through a damp sinking and senescence, and past this year's nests all open to view. And in what the poet John Clare describes as 'the doubting light'. He wrote an everlasting circle book called *The Shepherd's Calendar*, but his idiot publisher complained of its realities. There's no avoidance of these in the Faith-According-to-November, I tell the congregation. The countryside may be running down but we have to stir ourselves up. It says so here – 'Stir up the wills of thy faithful people.' 'But', they protest, 'you say the year is at an end with young Andrew!' The year but not the circle. Every oak knows that. Round and round we all go, the living, the departed, the abundance, the dearth, the planets, the prayers, the holiness of things, all our new toys and comforts notwithstanding.

Visit Penguin on the Internet
and browse at your leisure

- preview sample extracts of our forthcoming books
- read about your favourite authors
- investigate over 10,000 titles
- enter one of our literary quizzes
- win some fantastic prizes in our competitions
- e-mail us with your comments and book reviews
- instantly order any Penguin book

and masses more!

'To be recommended without reservation ... a rich and rewarding on-line experience' – Internet Magazine

www.penguin.co.uk

READ MORE IN PENGUIN

In every corner of the world, on every subject under the sun, Penguin represents quality and variety – the very best in publishing today.

For complete information about books available from Penguin – including Puffins, Penguin Classics and Arkana – and how to order them, write to us at the appropriate address below. Please note that for copyright reasons the selection of books varies from country to country.

In the United Kingdom: Please write to *Dept. EP, Penguin Books Ltd, Bath Road, Harmondsworth, West Drayton, Middlesex UB7 0DA*

In the United States: Please write to *Consumer Sales, Penguin USA, P.O. Box 999, Dept. 17109, Bergenfield, New Jersey 07621-0120.* VISA and MasterCard holders call 1-800-253-6476 to order Penguin titles

In Canada: Please write to *Penguin Books Canada Ltd, 10 Alcorn Avenue, Suite 300, Toronto, Ontario M4V 3B2*

In Australia: Please write to *Penguin Books Australia Ltd, P.O. Box 257, Ringwood, Victoria 3134*

In New Zealand: Please write to *Penguin Books (NZ) Ltd, Private Bag 102902, North Shore Mail Centre, Auckland 10*

In India: Please write to *Penguin Books India Pvt Ltd, 706 Eros Apartments, 56 Nehru Place, New Delhi 110 019*

In the Netherlands: Please write to *Penguin Books Netherlands bv, Postbus 3507, NL-1001 AH Amsterdam*

In Germany: Please write to *Penguin Books Deutschland GmbH, Metzlerstrasse 26, 60594 Frankfurt am Main*

In Spain: Please write to *Penguin Books S. A., Bravo Murillo 19, 1° B, 28015 Madrid*

In Italy: Please write to *Penguin Italia s.r.l., Via Felice Casati 20, I–20124 Milano*

In France: Please write to *Penguin France S. A., 17 rue Lejeune, F–31000 Toulouse*

In Japan: Please write to *Penguin Books Japan, Ishikiribashi Building, 2–5–4, Suido, Bunkyo-ku, Tokyo 112*

In South Africa: Please write to *Longman Penguin Southern Africa (Pty) Ltd, Private Bag X08, Bertsham 2013*

BY THE SAME AUTHOR

Akenfield

'One of the most absorbing books that I have read in the last ten years. A penetrating, extraordinarily unprejudiced, yet deeply caring account of modern rural life in England' – Angus Wilson

A huge bestseller, Ronald Blythe's close-up of a Suffolk village has, for most readers, justified C. P. Snow's forecast that it would become a classic of its kind. Only a man born and bred in the country could, one feels, have extracted the confidences and revelations that fill these pages as a soldier, a farm labourer, a district nurse, and ex-army officer and other typical figures tell their personal stories.

'One of the most poignant and moving books which I have read in years' – J. H. Plumb

'Beautiful and near-classic study of England in microcosm'
– *Sunday Times*

The Penguin Book of Diaries

'I never travel without my diary. One should always have something sensational to read on the train' – Oscar Wilde

Comical, confessional, gossipy, profound, absurd – the diarist's range is that of life itself. And diaries can be simultaneously a public record and a private room, a secret liason to be openly shared, a daily way of defeating the great victor, time.

Ronald Blythe introduces this wonderful anthology with an essay on the diarist's ambivalent art. He gives us gems from the journals of the famous and the unknown, personalities as various as Johnson, Darwin, Hardy, Evelyn Waugh and Virginia Woolf. Each contributor is introduced with a witty and scholarly portrait. They all share a passionate curiosity about the world and a particular genius for writing that catches the magic of the moment.

'There is much to enjoy . . . a rich kaleidoscope of British life over the last five centuries' – *Sunday Times*